More Blessed Than Kings

ESSAYS ON

CERTAIN MINOR CHARACTERS

IN THE FOUR

GOSPELS

MORE BLESSED THAN KINGS

by

VINCENT P. McCORRY, S.J.

The Newman Press

Westminster, Maryland

1954

Imprimi potest: Gulielmus F. Maloney S.J.
Praepositus Provincialis
Provinciae Marylandiae

Nihil obstat: Eduardus A. Cerny, S.S., D.D.
Censor Librorum

Imprimatur: Franciscus P. Keough, D.D.
Archiepiscopus Baltimorensis
die 23 Septembris 1954

FOR

my two Marthas and two Marys

whose names are

KATE   IRENE   MAY   FLORENCE

with endless gratitude

CONTENTS

Prologue

MORE BLESSED THAN MANY

In the tenth chapter of his first letter to the Christians of the ancient city of Corinth the redoubtable St. Paul, in his normally vigorous fashion, is busily trying to shield his yet tender flock from what we would now term the occasions of sin. The little Christian nucleus in that bustling Greek city must have been sorely tried as they struggled to lead a Christian life in the soft, pagan atmosphere of old Corinth. Worst of all, it must have been for them an attractive and recurrent temptation to relax the protective safeguards that shielded them from the comfortable but unlovely ways of the pagan life which they had renounced in Baptism. Such temptation will surely come, says Paul; and he urges his laboring Corinthians to learn strength from the disastrous follies of the Jews of days gone by. Paul cites from the Old Testament three striking punishments with which God rewarded the backsliding and idolatries and the bitter complainings of the ancient Jews, and he warns: *When all this happened to them, it was a symbol; the record of it was written as a warning to us.* *

* From the New Testament in the translation of Msgr. Ronald Knox, Copyright 1944, Sheed & Ward, Inc., New York. All New Testament citations are from Msgr. Knox' translation.

We Christian folk who live so many long centuries after Paul and his Corinthians may very justly seek in the inspired word of God the same warning and instruction and inspiration which they found in it. There is this notable and natural difference, however, between our situation and that of Paul's early converts from Judaism: for us, the center and heart of Scripture is no longer the Old Testament, but the four Gospel accounts of the birth, life and death of God's Son made man. The good news of the Gospel will always be the best news there is for the sincere follower of Christ.

The Gospel story sets before us an amazingly wide and rich cast of characters. There are kings and priests and criminals and newlyweds and day laborers and babies and soldiers and swindlers; there are men and women, good and bad, old and young. Inevitably and most properly, our loving attention fastens most closely on the towering central Person, that Jesus, God's Son and Mary's, who to us is everything, who is in very deed our way, our whole truth, our complete life. Our attention goes next to those compelling people who stand most closely grouped about our Lord, whether for weal or for woe: His utterly lovely Mother, the splendid man who was His foster father, His close friends like Peter and Magdalen, His final enemies like Judas and Pilate. But then, ranked more or less loosely in a wider circle about the exalted central Figure, there stand a small army of persons and characters who would be termed supernumerary in any story but the Gospel story.

These people of lesser importance in the Gospel narrative are certainly not supernumerary in the sense of being superfluous. The Holy Spirit has recorded them imperishably in a deed or a word or even a blunder; and the Holy Spirit has reminded us through Paul that *all* of this is written for our good. Besides, did not our Lord Himself suggest, at least by implication, that all those who with their own eyes saw Him and with their own ears heard Him were more blessed than many prophets and kings? *Then, turning to His own disciples, He said, Blessed are the eyes that see what you see; I tell you, there have been many prophets and kings who have longed to see what you see, and never saw it, to hear what you hear, and never heard it.* Of those whose mortal lives touched, however slightly, upon the mortal life of Christ Jesus, some were good, some were bad; some believed in Him, some did not; some, like the Good Thief, made a noble end; for others, like poor Judas, it would have been better if they had never been born. Yet all of these, because they stand for a moment silhouetted in the Light of the World, command our instant attention. At least in the order of external, visible fact, they were more fortunate than prophets. They were objectively more favored than kings. They were in some sort luckier than we.

In the pages that follow we will single out certain of the lesser Gospel characters for reflective and, we hope, profitable attention. One by one or group by group we will call some relatively unimportant people from the motley evangelical crowd in which they stand. There is a certain justice, we feel, in our being taught by rather unimportant people. *Pares cum paribus,* as the old Latin tag ran: Birds of a feather *should* flock together.

"In the days when Herod was king of Judaea, there was a priest called Zachary . . ."

LUKE 1:5

I

THE FATHER OF THE BAPTIST

We who insist on making mistakes can always learn from one who had to learn the hard way.

When Matthew, Mark, Luke and John sat down to write the good news with which they were burning and bursting, they made characteristically different beginnings to the story they had to tell. Matthew, the typical Jew, began with the patriarch Abraham. Mark, the voice of Peter, began with the voice of the prophet Isaias. John, the beloved disciple, began with God Himself. But Luke the doctor began with a priest. In order to introduce us to Christ the Messias, Luke introduces us to Zachary the priest.

The Jewish priesthood was a very different institution from the Christian priesthood that we know today. For one thing, the sacred office—and it *was* a sacred office—was hereditary: a man became a priest by being born of a descendant of Aaron and of the tribe of Levi. Vocation was then a simple thing, for it came by being born, free from technical impediments, of a priestly father. Certain consequences naturally flowed from such an uncomplicated arrangement. It followed that the Jewish priesthood was numerous: Zachary was one among some twenty thousand priests in a population that probably did not exceed five million. It followed likewise and necessarily that the Jewish priest was not celibate. For another thing, being a priest seems to have been very much in the nature of a part-time job, and a not very demanding one, at that. Certainly, as far as the principal work of Temple service was concerned, a Jewish priest worked one week twice a year. Nevertheless, the Jewish priesthood shared at least one external characteristic with the Christian priesthood: it was a privileged and respected institution. Zachary was reverend not only in years but in position. Our Lady's kinswoman Elizabeth had made a highly satisfactory marriage.

Highly satisfactory, that is, in every sense but one. Like countless women of almost every age in history but ours, the Jewish maiden ardently desired a husband for her bed chiefly in order that she might have a child for her crib; and in that terribly primary and primal sense, Elizabeth had made a marriage that was no marriage. She suffered the galling, humiliating sorrow of sterility, and years since, now, she and her husband, no longer young, had bidden farewell to the last, lingering hope for a baby. They spoke of it no more. Zachary was well accustomed to the gentle, defeated sadness that always looked out of Elizabeth's eyes and sometimes spoke in her voice.

It may have been in what we would call late summer of a certain significant year that there fell the time for Zachary's semi-annual week of service in the Temple of Jerusalem. The Jewish priests seem to have lived, for the most part, in towns within a short distance of the Holy City, and so it may have been on a hot Friday morning, when the first grapes hung ripe and purple on the vines and the golden wheat swayed ready for harvest, that old Zachary waved goodbye to Elizabeth and started slowly down the sloping path that led from their mountain village into the main road to Jerusalem. The priest's week of service in the Temple began on the Sabbath evening, and Zachary would suitably arrive in the holy place well before the evening sacrifice which ushered in the Sabbath.

The duties of the Temple priests were not more onerous than the period of their service. There were four chief sacerdotal tasks, and they were daily assigned by lot. The Temple priests offered the holocaust, the morning and evening burnt offering that was Israel's daily act of sacrifice; they trimmed and cared for the seven-branch candlestick which stood in the sacred antechamber to the Holy of Holies; they weekly renewed the twelve loaves of ceremonial bread which, representing the twelve tribes of Israel, rested on a golden table in the same antechamber; and— most coveted task of all—they daily burnt the fragrant incense on the golden altar in the same holy place. Only once in his lifetime did each priest offer the incense; having once performed the sacred rite, he was forever excluded from the drawing of lots for this prize.

We are twice assured that Zachary was an old man. All his priestly life he had taken part in the drawing, at first dawn, for the offering of incense. Is it conceivable that old Zachary had said farewell to this hope as he had bidden a long farewell to another? The lined and bearded face, gentle and wise and grave, must have been a study as Zachary—*haud sine Numine: not without the divine assist-*

ance—held at last in his trembling hand the cherished designation of God. We may imagine the profound absorption with which the old priest donned the special white ceremonial robe and moved slowly to the supreme priestly act of his life. Yet one thought, apparently, did not occur to his meditation. It is strange, perhaps; but he was old, and tired, and had grown unused to fair hope.

The cold ashes from the evening before had been swept from the golden altar of incense, the fresh new burning coals had been spread. The silver trumpets had spoken, and the priests, the men and the women of Israel stood silent and expectant in their separate courts. Zachary, robed in spotless white linen, holding before him in both hands a golden saucer of incense, walked gravely around the huge, richly embroidered tapestry which hung before the holy place, and stepped into the sanctuary. He advanced to the altar of incense, stood for a moment in a kind of rapture, then swiftly spread the incense on the live coals. The sweet gray clouds billowed upward from the altar, Zachary raised his eyes—and looked straight into the flashing countenance of a bright angel.

The Jewish people, for all their ancient and intimate converse with God, were flatly afraid of celestial apparitions. They were firmly convinced that to see God, or any visitant from the courts of God, was to die, and the Jews of old had no more appetite for dying than most of us have today. Zachary stood petrified in the presence of the angel; he simply waited for his heart to stop beating and his knees to buckle under him. But already, and quite calmly, the angel was speaking. The quiet, deliberate words crackled through Zachary's numb mind, and when the angel had done, one incredible sentence kept pounding in his head: *Thy wife Elizabeth is to bear thee a son.* The old man stared miserably at the shining vision. He thought: *Elizabeth? A son? But—* The *But,* black and enormous, swelled behind Zachary's eyes until it exploded, and the fragments of his incredulity dripped wretchedly from his lips: *By what sign am I to be assured of this? I am an old man now, and my wife is far advanced in age.* The angel's answer was icy cold with dignity: *My name is Gabriel.* . . . Zachary receives his sign, big, clear, palpable, paralyzing; the brief vision fades; the old man stumbles out of the sanctuary and dumbly turns toward the restless, now impatient crowd.

It is conceivable that speechless Zachary has something quite vital to say to anyone who has ears to hear.

Let us begin by asking: What was the matter with the good man whom the Gospel specifically describes as being well approved in God's sight? Where did Zachary make his mistake? What did he do that was so terribly wrong? True, he doubted; the priest of Israel questioned the sacred word, angelically transmitted, of the God of Israel. And yet one's instinctive sympathy goes out to an old man whose credulity wavered when he was suddenly presented with what must have seemed a very tall tale, even coming, as it did, from an accredited messenger of Omnipotence. Indeed Zachary acted very naturally. But it would seem that on occasion the God who made us, adopted us into His divine family and revealed Himself to us, expects us to act very supernaturally.

The point is that at a critical moment in his life, Zachary

failed in supernatural faith. But this allegation has to be explained.

To say that old Zachary failed in supernatural faith is, of course, not at all to say that this good man suddenly became an agnostic or a heretic or a sceptic with regard to divine revelation. Zachary was a Jew and a priest. He had been nurtured on the revealed word of God, his whole life was built on revelation; indeed, at the very moment of his doubt he was busily and reverently engaged in an authentic, external act of faith. It may be taken as certain that never, in all his long years, had the slightest doubt about God's revelation of Himself crossed Zachary's mind. In all probability, no frame of mind would have been more abhorrent to Zachary's whole nature than religious scepticism. In the fundamental sense, therefore, of a formal intellectual assent to the whole of duly revealed divine truth, Zachary's supernatural faith was above reproach.

Furthermore, it simply is not reasonable to suppose that Zachary's lapse of faith meant that he really doubted the capacity or competence of Almighty God the Creator so to temper ordinary biological laws as to permit an elderly couple to generate a child. Medical history does not fail to record such genial surprises, and although doctors may tend to raise an eyebrow at these eventualities, they show no inclination to explain them by appealing either to the supernatural or even the preternatural. In other words, a Jewish priest, reared, so to speak, on the miraculous, ideally conditioned to think of marvels as almost routine operation for the Most High, and distinctly acquainted through Scripture with precisely this sort of wonder—such a man, we say, would be the very last to doubt God's com-

petence to perform what would certainly seem a quite
minor miracle.

Well, then, what *was* the nature of Zachary's fall from
grace in the area of faith?

What Zachary doubted was neither God nor that God
could give him a son. What he doubted was that God
would. In other words, he believed in God and in God's
power. He just didn't especially believe in God's love. In a
technical formula, Zachary's faith was simply deficient in
the very exact sense that it lacked something; and what it
lacked was confidence. Like many a worse and many a
better man, Zachary was in effect a profound pessimist: he
did not completely *trust* his Father, God.

Like many a worse and many a better man? Let us consider.

One feels a powerful urge to resort to a risky superlative, but we shall be wary, and merely propose that *one*
of the most common and disastrous failings of perfectly
good people who sincerely want to love and serve God is
a deep-rooted lack of real confidence in God. The faith of
such distressed and uncertain Christians is like Zachary's:
it is there, but it is narrow, it is timid, it is not very sunny.
We who are Catholics, for example, certainly *believe* a
wide range of propositions, some of which go far beyond
the bounds of the Apostles' Creed. The sons and daughters of Holy Mother Church sometimes seem inclined to
credit the latest visions and ecstasies of the most palpable
neurotic, sometimes appear pathetically eager to endorse
and venerate bleeding statues, weeping pictures and falling rose petals. We believe with a vengeance, we believe
anything and everything, we believe left and right. The

only thing we do not completely believe is that God loves us; and so we do not pass serenely and easily from day to day, and from task to task, and from ease to pain and to sorrow and to death, because we do not rest confidently and trustingly in the strong love of God for us. Who believes with the most iron, unshakable faith, that God loves *him*; him, personally; him with all his foolish faults and wicked deeds upon his head; that God loves him with such a fierce and burning love that He will spare nothing, that He will do anything to prove that mighty love? In a word, which of us trusts God utterly, blindly, furiously, unshakably?

It is possible, of course, to supply a fairly comfortable answer to all these questions. Why, naturally, I trust God. I certainly hope to obtain pardon of my sins and life everlasting, and in the meantime—well, things are tough everywhere. I had a rough day yesterday, and today will be just as bad, and tomorrow, unquestionably, will be worse. Still, God is the boss, and I'll certainly go along with Him, especially since there's not much else I can do. God is very good, even though He does move in extremely mysterious ways, and why all this fuss about trust in God, anyhow? Of course, I trust Him; can't you hear me saying so?—Yes, good friend, we can hear you saying so, and forgive us if we modestly suggest that, like Shakespeare's lady, you do seem to protest too much. You are like many more of us: you trust God theoretically, you trust God verbally, you trust God according to strict limitations and specifications. And the question returns for all of us: Do we trust God actually, uncompromisingly, totally?

And, indeed, many an honest Christian soul would, upon

reflection, freely admit that he experiences a real interior difficulty in this whole matter of trusting God. The argument goes like this. Very well, God is good, and God loves us. No doubt God loves us so much that, as has been said, He will spare nothing on our behalf, He will do anything for us. All very fine. But if God will do *any*thing for me, why doesn't He do *some*thing for me: namely, this that I so terribly and painfully want at this moment? I want my mother to live; I want to succeed in my work; I want to be free of this worry; I want my dear love warm in my arms; I want to make an honest dollar; I want my little girl to recover her perfect sight; I want this dreadful pain to be not cancer—O God! not cancer; I want what I want, and I want it now, and if only I get it, I will always have such confidence in God, I will always trust Him so utterly!

Like every true cry of the anguished human heart, this cry is pitifully understandable. When the heart is wrung, the mind will stumble. We are sincere enough. We just do not perceive that although we are crying, we are not praying. We do not see that we are making an act of petition, but not an act of hope. It escapes us that we are arranging to trust God our Lord, not on the basis of His word, but on the basis of His performance.

And so we come laboriously to the ultimate explanation of our frequent failure to trust our loving God as we ought. It is that we are not actually attached to the Divine Will. We find ourselves so often in a set of circumstances where we fiercely desire one thing and where God, to all appearances, intends something quite different. We then suffer a well-founded suspicion that it is God's will, and not ours, which will finally be done. We don't like that. On succeeding occasions we naturally experience a profound distrust —never, of course, acknowledged, and perhaps never really faced—of Divine Providence and Its arrangements for us and the universe, especially for us. Gradually and imperceptibly we begin to doubt that our dear will, in relation to God, ever *will* be done. By that time we have arrived exactly at the position of old Zachary. We believe in God, we know all that He could do; we are just quietly and firmly convinced that He will *not* do this or that for *us*. For His special friends, yes; for St. Margaret Mary and Francis Xavier and the Little Flower and Mother Cabrini and the College of Cardinals, yes; but for me? Don't be silly. Why should He?

So our vaunted trust in God ends in moulting self-pity. Our faith is deficient because it lacks confidence. Our confidence is weak because we do not love God enough to prefer His will to ours. And we suddenly realize, perhaps with a start of surprise, that the three theological virtues are amazingly and intricately interwoven in the human soul. We abruptly perceive that the only way you can really have complete faith, hope or charity is, as people say nowadays, as a package.

Priest Zachary asked for a sign, and afterwards he could hardly have had much room for complaint, because he certainly got his sign. It was not an especially pleasant sign, but it was a solidly convincing one. We, who follow so long after and have seen so many more signs of God's sheltering and possessive love, ought really to labor at the cultivation of a faith which includes a most stalwart confidence, and a confidence which rests on a sturdy, practical love of the sort that staunchly prefers the Divine Will to our own. In a word, let us often ask our loving and generous Lord, who is emphatically eager to grant this request, for the package.

"She cried out with a loud voice . . . How have I deserved to be thus visited by the mother of my Lord?"

LUKE 1:42-43

II

ELIZABETH

Our Lady's kinswoman was amazing. She actually thought another woman was more important than herself.

There are a host of women in the Gospel story. They are a strikingly assorted group, too. They range in age, that tender female point, from the prophetess Anna to the little daughter of Jairus, in virtue from the shining Mother of our Lord to the much-married Samaritan woman, in attractiveness from Magdalen to the loud-mouthed portress who gave poor Peter such a bad time on the first Holy Thursday night. It would be next to impossible to imagine the Gospel narrative without the memorable representatives of the gentler sex who crowd the sacred pages. The Gospel world is by no means a man's world. The men may play the major parts—always excepting, of course, the utterly unique role of the Mother of God—but it is not infrequently the women who have the last word or do the last deed; as notably and nobly on Calvary. Now of all the women mentioned in the four Gospels, the chronological first is our Lady's kinswoman, priest Zachary's wife, she who became the mother of John the Baptist. Her name was Elizabeth. The name meant *God the faithful One.*

From the opening chapter of St. Luke's Gospel we learn not a little about this lady, Elizabeth. She was elderly, as Zachary insisted in his bad moment. She had suffered from life-long sterility. She was a good and religious woman. Above all, Elizabeth was related to our Lady and so to our Lord Himself. The precise degree of that blood relationship cannot now be determined. Some have thought that Mary and Elizabeth were born of sisters, and so were first cousins. Others, having in mind the sharply different ages involved, have suggested that Elizabeth was our Lady's aunt. In any event, Elizabeth was related in blood to the central Family of all time.

We may guess with what amazement and anxiety the wife of Zachary welcomed home her speechless husband after his week of Temple service. Laboriously he set before her in writing the stupendous experience he had had. Elizabeth, good woman, was probably little inclined to doubt her man's story; in any event, his anguished, still unaccustomed struggle to communicate with her would have shaken the incredulity of a professional sceptic. Besides, Elizabeth's own pathetic longing for a child would have disposed her to eager belief in her husband's heavenly visitant. The weeks passed. Upon a day, the wife of the old priest whispered to him that her name, Elizabeth, was found true at last, that now, in very deed, God was being for them the faithful One. Zachary, proud and humbled and choked with gratitude, made his silent prayer of thanks. His wife withdrew even from the mild bustle of their mountain village life, hugging to her heart her baby and her secret and her joy, shielding them all from idle, peering eyes.

Yet, strangely enough, Elizabeth's most exalted hour had not yet arrived and, strangely also, for that hour she would not have to await the birth of her son. Gabriel and God's mighty will had been busy in another place and with another woman and with another new Infant. At the end of Gabriel's joyous labor in that other place he had dropped a delicate hint; but no hint could be too subtle for the matchless fineness of the young woman who listened to him in gentle rapture. Not many days after, the lovely, smiling girl from Nazareth—and was she accompanied in this journey, one wonders, by her own mother, Anne?—hurried lightly up the path that led to the house of priest Zachary and stepped into the arms of her kinswoman.

So to Elizabeth came her great moment. Perhaps Zachary saw her transfigured, tear-wet face over Mary's shoulder as the elder woman held the young girl in her strong embrace, perhaps he heard the ringing, golden words that burst from her lips: *Blessed art thou among women, and blessed is the fruit of thy womb.* At last Elizabeth stood back and held Mary at arm's length before her. She spoke more slowly now, and in her voice there was a great wonder as she asked her noble question: *How have I deserved to be thus visited by the mother of my Lord?* Elizabeth waited for no answer to her question, nor shall we. For it is not a question that Elizabeth has given us. It is an answer to a question.

The problem to which Mary's kinswoman quite unconsciously provided a practical answer is a very real and fairly urgent problem for anyone who genuinely ambitions an authentic Christian life in the very real sense of a life actually planned and lived according to *all* the moral principles laid down by Christ our Lord, whether that life be lived in or out of the priesthood or the cloister. The problem is: What should be my general and initial attitude, all other considerations apart, toward those varied, countless people whose lives somehow or other, sometime or other, and more or less closely, impinge upon my life? Speaking most generally, how should I think of and act toward others? St. Ignatius Loyola formulates one answer to the question in the course of the rules which he left for his Jesuit family. The founder of the Society of Jesus bids his sons ever to yield to others the better and more desirable part of anything, "esteeming all *in their hearts* as their superiors." The directive happens to be a rule of a particular religious order, but the fact is, at the moment, inconsequential; what the rule enunciates is a moral principle of Christianity. Our Blessed Lord repeatedly insisted that His sincere followers would be the servants of all, would steadfastly seek the lowest place, would earnestly pray for those who persecute them. In a word, Christ our Lord recommended that we be humble.

This business of being humble, not in the genial sense of splendidly deprecating our own unquestionable achievements and excellences, but in the appallingly practical sense of treating other people as if they were really and actually superior to us, is not a procedure that recommends itself to many. Theoretical humility is a rather pleasant thing, it is a sweet idea, but anything like a realistic habit of acting toward others as if they were superior to us must surely be ridiculously impractical, chiefly because it is bound to become, in many cases, most—well, most *humiliating*. It is all very well for the high-born priest's wife,

Elizabeth, to regard plain Mary of Nazareth as her superior, because, as everyone knows, Mary, for all her being the carpenter's wife, really was more important than Elizabeth. As for St. Ignatius and the Jesuits, such smart men have surely, in four hundred years, worked out some cozy solution to *that* little knot in their daily lives. Are we to suppose for a moment that Christ would seriously want us to treat our colored cook as if she were our superior? And if so, what is the world going to come to?

Yes. Yes, that is *exactly* what Christ seriously wants us to do. It is strange, it is disturbing, but it is true. And if we who profess Christ's name would really try to do something of that sort, the world might indeed come to a *very* pretty pass. We all might begin to get along quite beautifully together. We might even start to be relatively and surprisingly happy.

Admittedly, however, this matter is not quite so simple as all that. For instance, the sincere question might be asked: Is this principle of looking up to all others as our betters really practical in the rudimentary sense of being regularly *possible,* of being capable of application and performance in the actual contacts of daily existence? How *can* I regard the janitor as my superior if I own the whole building which he janitors? Before attempting any detailed response to this troublesome question, let us at once recall a fact and a manifest conclusion from that fact. The fact is that Christ our Lord did command this type and degree of self-abasement. *If anyone has a mind to be the greatest, he must be the last of all, and the servant of all. . . . When thou art summoned, go straight to the lowest place and sit down there. . . . No difference is to be made, among you,*

*between the greatest and the youngest of all, between him
who commands and him who serves. . . . Why, then, if I
have washed your feet, you in your turn ought to wash
each other's feet.* So much for the fact. The manifest conclusion from the fact is that if Christ our Lord commanded
us to do something, it must really be at least *possible* to
do just that. As old St. Jerome remarks somewhat dryly,
"We must realize that what Christ commands is not the
impossible, but the perfect: *non impossibilia . . . sed per-
fecta.*" So, then, it certainly must be possible to look upon
assorted, unlikely people as our betters.

It must be obvious that there is something very real
which this challenging precept of humility does *not* mean.
It does not change or qualify the existent, external order
of reality: one person continues to be the official, external
and very visible superior or owner or boss, and the other
person continues to be the external subject or tenant or
employee. The virtue of humility does not require that I
give my building to the janitor or prepare the cook's break-
fast. A humble attitude toward others is primarily just
that: an attitude, a habitual, interior frame of mind, a
tenaciously held conviction. Secondly, that attitude then
manifests itself in reasonable and respectful and profoundly humane treatment of all other people without
exception. Incidentally, of course, the whole virtue has
nothing whatever to do with the trivial and unsupernatural
phenomenon of liking or disliking any particular person.

Since the business of maintaining such a modest and
respectful demeanor toward others is obviously difficult,
we may aid ourselves by inquiring whether there be any
natural considerations which would encourage this humble

frame of mind. Someone has said that there is no such thing as a completely homely woman: every woman has at least one beautiful feature. Is it extravagant for me to suspect in some analogous way that every human being may well be my better in some one perhaps quite hidden respect? Very little of the complete truth about people is immediately visible; entertaining an angel unawares is one of the likeliest possibilities on the face of the earth. How deeply good men and women are, how hard they really do try, how keenly and how frequently they suffer, in how many faults they contract little or no culpability, against what crushing odds they are struggling—very little of all this moving truth about human beings ever shows on the surface. Priests are supposed to know how frighteningly evil men and women can be; but it remains one of the solid joys of the priesthood that we also come to realize just how astonishingly and thoroughly good a child of Adam quite frequently is. Never despair of a priest. He may yet be shamed into holiness—by his penitents. But one need not be a priest in order to learn a certain caution in judging others by surface indications. Ordinary common sense plus a very little experience ought to suggest that we run a considerable risk when we start to look down on anyone at all. I recall that as a new and bewildered novice in religious life I finally found to my great satisfaction one somnolent, drowsy-looking and myopic individual whom I could safely patronize. I was somewhat disconcerted to discover subsequently that the obvious sleep-walker used to read Homer in the original Greek by way of recreation. It was quite a shock, thank God.

Nevertheless, anything like a habitual reverence for

others as our betters must rest chiefly on purely supernatural considerations, and of these there are a number
which make very much for the purpose.

To begin with, every human being is the direct handi-
work of God, every living person is made in the image and
likeness of the Divine Majesty. No man, woman or child
is an accident; every single individual is the concrete realization of a divine purpose and plan, is the termination or
direct result of a perfectly free and volitional divine act.
Moreover, every human being *reflects* divinity. I may consider, if I feel so inclined, that the image of God in this
particular person is quite thoroughly blurred and distorted,
but I had better go cautiously, even so. Am I really in a
position to decide which human person most accurately
reflects the God whom I have never seen and of whom I
must even speak in the most halting, remote and fairly
inaccurate human terms? *Nigra sum, sed formosa,* is the
mysterious remark of the beloved in the Song of Songs:
I am black, but beautiful. Can I *prove* that a Negro or a
Chinaman is wrought less to the image of God than I
am? Indeed, if I pursue this fruitful line of thought long
enough, I may begin to look with considerable reverence
upon that bent, wooly head while the busy, black hands
shine my shoes. Am I *sure* which one of us is fashioned
more truly in the image of God?

Next, there comes the whole pertinent and explosive
supernatural truth called the Incarnation. God our Lord is,
of course, the greatest democrat in all human history, for
not only did He truly become, in every sense that does not
imply sin, a man among men, but He became a plain man
among plain men for the sake of absolutely *all* men with-

out exception. It makes bad news for all the many Christian snobs and all the "exclusive" Catholics, but almighty God has adequately demonstrated that He is, in every fine sense of the word, incorrigibly vulgarian. Our God has chosen to wear this muddy vesture of human flesh, He has hidden His splendescent divinity under mortal sweat and honest human dirt. Not content with becoming one of us, He became a very plain one of us: a carpenter, a workingman, a small-town fellow. And on top of all this, our Incarnate God moved serenely through His mortal life constantly showing an unmistakable preference for precisely the sort of people whom we would unhesitatingly patronize. He lived almost entirely among the poor, He regularly associated with unfragrant fishermen, He shocked everybody by calmly making an Apostle of a despised tax collector, He repeatedly occupied Himself with children, He warmly praised a poor widow for an infinitesimal almsdeed, He sang the praises of John the Baptist while John reposed in that most unselect of places, jail; He protected and encouraged and finally sanctified a lady of easy virtue, Mary Magdalen. Christ our Lord, *the radiance of His Father's splendor and the full expression of His being,* manifested a determined taste for what we might call low company. He was trying to convey to our dainty and discriminating and not too bright minds that if anything on the face of the earth is common and absolutely universal property, He is. The Incarnation is deplorably lacking in selectivity. It was and is for everybody.

Does all this rambling argument prove that I ought to be at least amenable to the notion of regarding others with profound respect and even of deferring to them as to my betters? No doubt the demonstration is not philosophically airtight, but a certain strong suggestiveness nevertheless floats through this Incarnational atmosphere. Christ our Lord did truly become man for the sake of the poor old duffer who is now feebly rattling around the room as I try to write, who will ineffectually wave a dust-cloth and push a dirty mop, and who will soon depart with my brand-new wastebasket (that essential for any writer) which he will only return to someone else's room. I will be glad, naturally, when the shabby old sweep shuts the door of my room upon himself; but I had better be extremely careful about shutting any doors on him. Christ loves him so much that He became man for him, and I simply am in no position to argue or assume that the Incarnation is more completely and truly successful for me than it is for him. In fact, the more I think of it . . .

Finally, every human being is a *de jure* temple or dwelling-place of the Holy Spirit, the third Person of the most blessed Trinity, that Holy Spirit who is both truth and love, who ever proceeds from the Father and the Son. The Latinism means, of course, that every human being *ought* to be a temple of the Holy Spirit. Now whether, in a particular case, the *de jure* situation is actually verified in fact —*that* is something which I cannot possibly know short of downright confession on the part of the individual, and people do not make a habit of confessing their sins to passers-by or even to casual acquaintances. There is a gentle old story of an aged religious priest who always tipped his biretta to the novices, explaining that he really wasn't saluting the novice, but the novice's guardian angel. The suggestion is a richly salutary one. My best assumption with regard to anyone is that that person is actually at this moment a living temple of the Holy Spirit; and I may caution myself to bear myself reverently toward that silent, invisible, majestic Presence. There should not really be any special difficulty, even for wonderful me, about treating the Holy Spirit as my better.

It requires no particular gift of either intelligence or observation to find something in another person which will encourage me to look down on him. I rate no special credit for noting that I am better educated than this factory worker, that my hands are cleaner than the plumber's, that I am a more accomplished public speaker than the average truck-driver. What really does require a little intelligence, a little reflection and a deal of downright moral goodness is to perceive the distinct possibility that the factory worker and the plumber and the truck-driver may be better men than I am, and, in the penetrating sight of God our Lord, a vast deal more truly important than I; and then to treat them accordingly.

If Elizabeth, with a little lift from the Holy Spirit, could see and acknowledge the Mother of God in the simple young girl from Nazareth, we, with just a little of the same divine prodding, ought to be able to see that we walk the streets and sit in buses surrounded by children of God and heirs of heaven, and to adjust ourselves nicely to our surroundings. *Come, Holy Spirit!*

"The shepherds said to one another, Come, let us make our way to Bethlehem, and see for ourselves . . ."

LUKE 2:15

III

THE SHEPHERDS

The angelic chorus swelled majestically, and the ragged shepherds came running—perhaps to tell us something?

Literary people, who are, in general, a mad but rather appealing lot, cannot have done admiring certain passages in the four Gospels. Ordinarily, the earnest, workaday believer in Christ our Lord does not trouble his head over the stylistic beauties of Matthew, Mark, Luke and John, for he knows that in listening to the Evangelists he is really listening to the mighty murmuring of the Holy Spirit, and he is tolerably well content to lay aside his newspaper and turn off the radio and walk out on television simply in order to come into direct contact with absolute and infallible truth. Yet there are passages in the Gospels which, as often as we read them, weave a kind of spell upon us, a spell not altogether due to the utter truth which is expressed. In such contexts we encounter that perfect wedding between substance and mode of expression, between exalted thought and exalted style, which constitutes the highest communication this side of the authentic mystical experience. Such a passage is, of course, St. Luke's account of the birth of our Lord.

But it is not the velvet beauty of this unforgettable narrative that we would like now to discuss. We would wish rather to note a curious point. The entire account of the first Christmas night occupies twenty verses at the beginning of Luke's second chapter. Of the twenty verses, four provide what we might call the historical background of the tremendous event. The following three verses, almost eerie in their nakedness, tell us of the actual birth of Jesus. The remaining thirteen verses are concerned with the surprised and the surprising group of men who were the first mortals to be informed of the Nativity. As the cigarette people would say nowadays, it's the Shepherds, four to one.

Everyone remembers what happened on that first starry Christmas night. When our Savior was born, Bethlehem and its people were more or less blissfully sleeping, but not everyone was sleeping. As always and everywhere in human affairs, while the majority of men turn them wearily to the balm of hurt minds and the great nourisher in life's feast, some few must continue to toil through the quiet hours of darkness. So it was with the little group of shepherds that night. We cannot be sure of the precise date of our Lord's birth, but at least it must have happened in a season of fair weather, for the flocks were being left out to pasture. Because of the constant threat of the wolf which was found everywhere in Palestine, and because of the monumental stupidity and helplessness of sheep, the shepherd was obliged to maintain a twenty-four hour guard over his flock while it lay in pasture, as distinct from the period, mentioned by our Lord in His parable, when the sheep were locked securely in the sheepfold.

So, on the first Christmas night, while men with easier jobs snored and tossed and muttered in sleep, a small group of sheep-herders stood watch over their drowsy charges on the slope outside Bethlehem town. Their work was the most exasperating sort of night labor. There was little to do, for the sheep were bedded down, huddled together for warmth and comfort, yet the Shepherds themselves could not risk sleep; they must watch endlessly for the vague, gray shadow that would slip cunningly into the very edge of the flock for one quick, silent slash at a wooly throat. The chilly hours passed, the stars wheeled overhead, the watch-fire was replenished, the silent men stood about the fire or drifted off in turn to walk another careful circle around the bedded flock. Those about the fire noticed with dull surprise that the crimson flames were growing pale. Dawn already? Would that all nights were as short as this one seemed to be! But then they were gaping at one another, all wide awake now, and those on their rounds were running toward the fire, and the whole hillside swam in a soft, bright splendor. They were plain men, these workers in the night, and their learning was precious little, but a thing or two they knew. They knew, for example, that they were not standing in the welcome light of an early dawn. They were now bathed in the Schechinah, the dread, awful brightness of God's actual presence. They stood shaking, waiting to die.

But the Shepherds did not die. Instead, they saw a bright, angelic presence and heard a warm, happy voice. It said, *Do not be afraid*. Then, like a shower of priceless silver, the good news came pouring down upon these ragged men and they heard themselves invited to the birthday party of the little Son of God. They stood rapt as the splendid chords of glory to God and peace on earth drenched the hillside with unearthly melody. And finally they were looking at one another in the ruddy light of the perfectly ordinary watch-fire, and once again they could see the stars overhead, especially one very bright one. Then these plain men did a good thing. Believing like children and quite unlike priest Zachary in all that the angel had said, they cheerfully left their flocks to the care of any unoccupied angel that might have been left around, and they came hustling and bursting into the stable-cave and to the sweet sight that prophets and kings and you and I would give years of our lives to have seen. *And so they went with all haste,* says St. Luke, enviously, *and found Mary and Joseph there, with the Child lying in the manger.*

Such is the story of the Shepherds. And the point of the story would seem to be that that is all there is to the story. We know nothing more about these simple herdsmen of a night than that they were invited to the crib of Christ, and that they came. How many there were, how old they were, whether one was a lad and one a very old man, what their names were, what became of them after that first Christmas night—to all these really pertinent questions we have no answers. The anonymous Shepherds come bursting into the Gospel story, they come running to the manger, they go happily and, it would seem, noisily back to their night's work, and as the rough, excited, kindly voices die away, and the striding figures melt into the darkness, we realize with a little pang that these hearty men have marched out of the Gospel into oblivion. We do not see them or hear them or hear of them again. That is precisely the point.

The importance of the Shepherds is their unimportance.

Importance is a curious thing. It is well worth thinking about, especially for anyone who professes the Christian philosophy of life. It is a problem for those who in any sense possess it, and a yet sharper problem for those who do not have it at all.

To begin with, every man who draws breath is ineluctably persuaded of his own uniqueness, and therein he is not altogether wrong. I may be the most ordinary individual on the face of the earth, but it is not my ordinariness that impresses me nearly as much as the startling fact of my individuality. I may not be much; but I am not you, I am not he or she or they. I am I, and on the whole I am glad of it. Moreover, I simply cannot persuade myself that I am utterly and absolutely inconsequential. I don't feel inconsequential. My body is a solid fact. My thoughts have a certain interest. My decisions have a cost or a recompense for me. My heartache is a real ache in a real heart, and it stabs me as no other heartache can. You may shout at me until the heavens split that I am nothing, that I do not amount to a hill of beans, that I am not worth the snap of a finger, and I will only stare bleakly back in a fog of incomprehension. I know that I am I, and I still feel a certain tenderness for me. Nor am I to be blamed for this. Significantly, the great commandment of fraternal charity only bids me love another as I love myself.

It follows, then, with utter naturalness and a sort of necessity, that every man wants to be somebody rather than nobody. He knows he *is* somebody; and when in the smallest way, the smallest number of his fellows unite to acknowledge that he is indeed somebody, the human heart tastes a simple, quite childlike gratification that is headier than rare wine. The more often Jones or Smith or Murphy is recognized as somehow special or outstanding, and the more numerous bystanders join in the roaring shouts of acclamation, the more joyously intoxicated will Jones or Smith or Murphy become. He is now a person of consequence, he has now achieved a certain importance: he is now *Mr.* Jones or *Boss* Smith or *Champ* Murphy and, hang it all, he's happy!

Could any tiny human drama or adventure be more understandable? But it is not the people who ever do attain any importance who concern us at this moment. We are thinking of those who never do. We want to talk about and maybe talk to the vast army of those earnest Christian men and women, husbands and wives and bachelors and spinsters and sometimes hardworking religious, who pass their whole lives without a single sip of the wine of importance, who are—possibly through no deliberate volition of their own—total abstainers from this heady vintage. We would like to speak, with profound respect, to all the shepherd-like people who will not even have in all their lives the one shining hour that the Shepherds had.

It is not our intention to question the true and ultimate value of any prominence that may be achieved in this miry world. We only wish to note that whatever the true worth of importance, most people don't have it. For every general there are so many buck privates, for every department head there are so many clerks, for every brain there are so many lamebrains, for every rich man there is such a host of the poor. Even in the world of religion there is only one bishop for many hustling parish priests, and when the celebrated preacher climbs confidently into the pulpit no one thinks of the scurrying Sisters and the sweating Brothers who polished the sanctuary and decorated the altar and taught the choir-children the *Come, Holy Ghost* with which they just brought down the flaming Spirit of Truth on the preacher's needy head. We ask: What can or should be said to the vast, swarming, toiling army of those who might be called quite truly and quite falsely the little people in the kingdom of God?

Three things should be said. First, the little people—and we beg to be forgiven a mere phrase of convenience; the reader must purge the expression of the slightest hint of condescension—the little people must be convinced that in their very unimportance they are well out of harm's way. Say what we will, a certain vague menace attaches to every form of prominence. There is a never-ending danger that the person of consequence will someday start to believe what he sees and hears. There is the constant and blood-curdling possibility that the important man will actually begin to suspect that he really is important. Something of Satan's own temptation must always attend upon high place. We have already suggested that any kind of notice is intoxicating. Add to that the giddiness which some people experience when they look down from an elevation, and we may readily conclude that it is quite a trick for highly placed personages to maintain that level-headed sobriety which both Peter and Paul recommend in their letters.

From all this real and prolonged danger obscure people are almost totally free. You can't fall far if you're already standing on the ground, and no one is apt to grow dizzy looking out the windows of the cellar unless it happens to be the wine-cellar, and that problem we're not discussing just now. Moreover, the little people should remember that importance is not only a vague danger but also a distinct burden. The whole pattern and structure of human responsibility is triangular, and the triangle rests not on its base but on its apex, the apex being the person finally in charge of any particular enterprise or matter. Thus every human being who heads anything of consequence is the point of an inverted triangle of responsibility, and that is one point which the obscure man or woman ought to be rather glad to miss. Unimportant people may not be often in the common eye, but they are not much in the common hair, either.

Secondly, it is not mere sentimentality to suggest that, other things being equal, the little ones of this world are rather specially dear to God. We have already noted the very particular attention paid by our Lord in His own lifetime to people whom others wouldn't have bothered about for a moment. He made the clearest revelation of Himself to the Samaritan lady who was not a lady at all, He performed one of His rarest miracles for the nameless widow of Naim, He outraged all the quality by having dinner with a queer collection of shady characters and down-and-outers. In His mystical life in the Church Christ our Lord shows exactly the same tendency toward intimacy with little people, and His Mother, if we may so put it, takes after Him. Paray-le-Monial, Lourdes, and Fatima are convincing examples of God's inclination to bypass bishops, theologians, movie stars and philanthropical millionaires when He has exceptional and urgent business on hand.

Personally, I count among God's closest friends the following people whom I have been fortunate enough to meet:
an elderly, arthritic nun who long ago landed in this country from Ireland, went directly from the dock to a large
convent, for the next fifty years cooked all the meals for a
numerous community, and who now feels guilty about the
good care she is getting when she can't do a tap of work;
a priest who has a slight stammer, who wears only second-
hand suits and cassocks, and who has devoted himself to
parish work among Negroes; a policeman who raised ten
children on one patrolman's salary and daily Mass and
Holy Communion; and a young truck-driver who is something of a contemplative. I have also met a few prima
donnas and assorted presidents of things, and even some
poets and politicians; but them I have happily forgotten.

The third and final reflection to be commended to the
little ones of this world is a notion which would be extremely risky if it were suggested to anyone else. It is this.
Unimportant people should not hesitate to believe that
they are really much nicer than important people. I suppose even lowly folk ought not to flirt habitually with
such a notion, but it is hard to see how anyone can doubt
the truth therein contained. Importance and high honor
are corruptive, as anyone must admit who knows anything
about human nature, the history of the Church and goings-
on in Washington, D.C. Any number of Very Important
Persons are also very admirable human beings, but, if they
will forgive me, they aren't as pleasant to have around as
five times as many little people. The voice of authority
tends to grow sharper and less pacifying the longer it continues to be the voice of the same individual, and that is

why Catholic Canon Law is never more sagacious than when it limits the term of office of most religious superiors. Since authority under such conditions is inextricably mixed up with the fine old adage that whatever goes up must come down, religious superiors are usually much slower than other V.I.P.'s to believe that either Rome or heaven or the American Constitution always speaks when they do. Still, even in the cloister, the most relaxed and most relaxing people are usually the lay Sisters and the coadjutor Brothers.

Of course, in the final analysis even the mere *fact* of importance is difficult to measure and assess. The Shepherds who knelt about the small Christ that Christmas night are for us today not only nameless but also featureless; and yet what prince in all history has become as famous as they? As long as there is a Christ-Mass the story of the Shepherds will be told, and as long as there shall be a Christmas crib, children will know who the Shepherds were. The forgotten herdsmen of a night are the remembered Shepherds of all the centuries to come. As usual, our Savior summed up in one brief sentence the whole meaning of the Shepherds and of all the little people who will ever be. *The last shall be first*, said Christ laconically. And of course they will be.

"And when the child Jesus was brought in by His parents . . . Simeon too was able to take Him in his arms . . ."

LUKE 2:27-28

IV

SIMEON

The younger can always learn from those who are older; and most of us are younger than the grand old man of Candlemas.

One of the acute problems of human beings is remembering. Remembering is a problem in a double sense; first,
because we too often remember what we ought to forget:
the harsh word, the unspeakable folly, the dear face, the
sweet, lost love; secondly, because we strongly tend to
forget what we ought to remember: a promise or an anni-
versary or a name. This double problem exists in the relationship between man and man and it exists in the more
primary relationship between man and God. There really
are things which God our Lord emphatically wants us to
forget, even though those poor psychopaths who make a
business of scruples will not entertain the idea for a
moment, and there are quite a lot of things which God
strongly wants us to remember. For example, God prefers
that we bear more or less steadily in mind the outstanding
or crucial blessings He has bestowed upon us: that I
married a truly wonderful girl or that I recovered my
threatened sight or that I am a priest forever according to
the order of Melchisedech. Now obviously, if a man can
forget God's richest blessings in the course of a single lifetime, a whole people will be extremely apt to forget the
wonderful deeds God wrought for their fathers a score of

generations ago. In the case of the Jews, His chosen people, almighty God took strong measures to ensure that they would not allow certain glorious or critical moments of their past to fall finally from mind. Such a moment was the wildly exciting and decisive time of the escape of Israel from the slavery of Egypt.

In one of those vast floods of migration which seem to have been a characteristic of the ancient Oriental world the people of Israel had drifted south and west into the pagan but friendly land of Egypt, and had firmly established themselves there. Apparently they had a rather pleasant time of it. They prospered and multiplied, and when one of their number, the first Biblical Joseph, actually became the prime minister to the ruling Pharaoh the people of Israel must have enjoyed a position of complete security and perhaps relative privilege. We know also that the Jews even liked the food in their new home; years later, during their nomadic desert life, they cannot stop talking about the excellent Egyptian cuisine, and especially about (of all things!) the fine Egyptian onions which they had so relished. However, there were surely many in Egypt who looked upon the meteoric rise of Joseph precisely as many in Victorian England regarded the career of Disraeli, and very soon after the death of Joseph and Joseph's Pharaoh there occurred that sharp change in political and popular feeling which has never ceased to menace and haunt the Jewish people. A wave of anti-Semitism swept over Egypt, typical repressive measures were invoked, the economic position of the Jewish group was dynamited, bloodshed— with Jews as victims—became more and more common-place, and finally the people of Israel were reduced to a position of downright slavery. At that moment there came striding into Egypt from the south, after a checkered career and a flaming vision, the extraordinary man called Moses.

Of the protracted and violent battle between Moses, Aaron and the God of Israel, on the one hand, and, on the other, Pharaoh and the Egyptian landowners, who hated to see a good thing like unlimited slave-labor slip through their fingers, you may read in the second book of the Old Testament. Pharaoh proved to be remarkably stubborn: he resisted nine different divine visitations which must have made life in Egypt a waking nightmare. Then, after a final, solemn warning, came the tenth and the last plague: in one night a destroying angel slew all the first-born of Egypt, *from the firstborn of Pharaoh, who sat on his throne, unto the firstborn of the captive woman that was in the prison, and all the firstborn of cattle.** In every patriarchal society an almost mystical significance attaches to the firstborn son, for this child, as the future head of the family, exercises a sort of limited priesthood. Pharaoh and the Egyptians, reeling under the most severe of all possible blows, swiftly capitulated. The people of Israel, loaded with legitimate spoil and delirious with the sweet air of freedom, marched triumphantly out of Egypt and slavery and a dark era in their history.

It was this miraculous escape, this hard-bought rescue engineered wholly by divine omnipotence, that God wished branded on the memory of Israel. So God meticulously

* From the Old Testament Vol. I in the translation of Msgr. Ronald Knox, Copyright 1948, Sheed & Ward, Inc., New York. All citations from the Old Testament are taken from Msgr. Knox' translation.

ordered the precise manner in which the sacred Passover should be annually observed in honor of the event. And in order that the memory of the escape from Egypt might be written not only in ceremony but in a living person, God now claimed as His own in a most specific way all the first-born sons of His chosen people: *Since the day when I struck all the firstborn of the land of Egypt, I have consecrated to myself all the firstborn of Israel, both man and beast. They are mine.* Since firstborn sons were therefore God's *property,* they had to be *bought back* from God in order that they might in any legitimate sense belong to their parents. This ceremony of redemption or re-purchase took place some forty days after the birth of the firstborn boy, and it was described as presenting the child to the Lord. For this ancient purpose, then, on the fortieth day after our Lord's birth, lovely Mary and good Joseph, carrying the Baby by turns, trudged happily to the great Temple of Jerusalem.

We will guess that Mary and Joseph—the Little One now resting like a star on Mary's breast—had just passed through the famed Gate Beautiful and had entered the Court of Women; that they stood for a moment looking about them, a most inconspicuous young couple with a new baby, when a very old man, standing some little distance from them, turned as with a start and looked hard at them. Surprised, as they probably always were by any special attention, Mary and Joseph exchanged an inquiring glance. Then they began to move across the Court. But the old man, now striding like a youth, bore down on them. He blocked their way, and, after one quick glance at the ancient face, all Mary's faint uneasiness vanished. The

venerable one was looking neither at her nor at Joseph.
His eyes were fixed almost hungrily on the Baby, and even
as Mary and Joseph watched, the old man's lips trembled,
and two great tears ran down the lined cheeks. With
utmost simplicity the patriarch held out his arms, and
without hesitation Mary put her Baby into them. Tired old
eyes rested peacefully on the tiny, rosy infant face. Then
the old man spoke. He spoke the gentle words which have
become the last prayer with which Holy Mother Church
in her liturgy bids farewell to each dying day: *Nunc dimit-*
tis. Ruler of all, now dost Thou let Thy servant go in peace,
according to Thy word; for my own eyes have seen that
saving power of Thine which Thou hast prepared in the
sight of all nations. This is the light which shall give revela-
tion to the Gentiles, this is the glory of Thy people Israel.
So spoke old Simeon. His is one of the great cries of con-
tentment in all literature.

We know a thing or two about this man Simeon. Oddly
enough, we do not know by way of explicit statement the
very first fact that we assume about him: that he was a
very old man. The assumption, however, is more than a
little reasonable in view of three highly suggestive points
which Luke does mention. We are told that Simeon
waited patiently for the appearance of the hope of Israel.
We learn that, according to a supernatural guarantee he
had received, *he was not to see death until he had seen*
that Christ whom the Lord had anointed. Finally, we have
the *Nunc dimittis,* a prayer which would sound somewhat
strange on youthful lips. Add to all this the responsible
voice of tradition, and we are adequately assured that we
may continue to refer to Simeon as the old man of Candle-

mas. As for character, Luke describes old Simeon by two adjectives which picture him as both interiorly and exteriorly admirable: he was profoundly just in heart, and exactly careful in religious observance; *an upright man of careful observance*, as Monsignor Knox so exactly translates. The second quality might itself explain the old man's presence in the Temple on the day of our Lord's presentation, but we are explicitly told that Simeon came to the Temple that day precisely as, years later, our Savior Himself would go into the desert: *led by the Spirit*.

What we know about this venerable man, however, is not nearly so important for our present intent as what we may very properly conclude from what we know of him. If, then, the shepherds spell out for us the importance of unimportance, old Simeon instructs us in the potency of patience.

Patience is a word of Latin origin, and it involves considerably more than keeping one's temper when a shoelace breaks. Not to make a song or a grammar lesson out of a minor matter, patience is one of those words, like *disaster* or *promotion* or *lost*, which are passive, not in form, but in their whole burden of meaning: such words do not suggest that someone is doing something, but that something is being done to someone. Patience, as a word, is an exceedingly passive word—and perhaps that is what deceives us: it means not only that something is being done to me, but that I either freely allow it to be done to me, or at least do not collapse under it or surrender to it. The word, in a word, means *endurance*.

Now we do not commonly speak of enduring good news or enduring success or enduring a superlative dinner or even of enduring a honeymoon. What a man is said to endure is something unpleasant: hard usage or poverty or sickness. If he bears such burdens with any kind of grace, he is said to be patient. If he bears such burdens with any kind of grace over a considerable period of time, he is sometimes said (however awkwardly) to possess the virtue of long-suffering. However, we wish to notice here a slightly different type of patience or endurance or long-suffering. It is difficult to put up with something unpleasant; but it can be exceedingly difficult to put up with nothing, when nothing happens to be exceedingly unpleasant. In clearer terms, one very notable variety of real and costly patience is the patience which waits with indomitable fortitude over a period of years for some grace, some blessing, some joy which is so much desired but so long deferred. A man in these circumstances may be otherwise quite comfortable, he may be free from notable mischance or worry or pain, but he longs eagerly for some good, a good that does truly mean his complete peace and real fruition, and such good is not granted him; yet he moves strongly and with a certain determined serenity from day to uneventful day, never doubting, since God is so loving, that at long last, somehow, somewhere, he will yet possess his heart's desire. Such a man is truly patient. Such a man is truly a good man. Such a man was Simeon, and such men and women should we Christians be. According to our Savior's somewhat mysterious dictate, we are all to possess our souls in patience.

It would be futile, and not particularly helpful, to attempt to enumerate the many good things which most of us have to await with considerable patience as we make our uncertain way through this world. Still, let us attempt a kind of formula. Those who in any sense endorse the name of Christ may be sure that they will have to wait patiently, and with greater or less long-suffering, for a quartet of blessings: for help, happiness, holiness and heaven.

The help which we must all patiently await is, of course, supernatural help. This is not at all to say that God our Lord delays for a moment the sufficient graces we need at any particular time. We mean only what is perfectly obvious: that God does not always immediately dispatch to us the kind of help we desire as soon as we desire it. In plain terms, the first kind of patience (in our present sense) which a Christian must exercise is patience with Divine Providence in the frequent event of what is popularly referred to as unanswered prayer. The problem is surely not acute when we ask God for fair weather tomorrow or for a raise in salary or that the Dodgers, those sainted men, may win the pennant. But when we beg our loving Lord for what will so indubitably make for his glory—that I may be delivered from the anarchy of my evil tendencies, that our local pastor may begin to worry less about paying bills and more about the spiritual welfare of the parish, that our little girl, stricken with polio, may not be crippled for life—it is when such unselfish and wholesome petitions go begging for months and years that the problem of patience with God arises. In this earnest pleading we cannot help but feel keenly that what we ask is so *good*; yet the days pass, and the heavens are blank. God gives no sign. We look desperately at the crucifix, at the statue of the Sacred Heart, at the sweet image of our Lady, and they are all as silent and serene, as impassive and unmoved, as if there were no tears in our eyes, no ache in our hearts. Like Simeon, who only wanted to look upon the face of Christ, we want nothing but what is good. Like Simeon, we have to wait for it. Will we, like Simeon, wait patiently?

When we suggested, a moment ago, that the average Catholic or Christian must, in the second place, wait patiently for happenings, we were not trying to be mysterious, but were only yielding to the twittering, tattle-tale temptation of alliteration. The notion involved is again sufficiently obvious. The very first characteristic of the lives of most of us is that they are so completely ordinary. We rise unwillingly each morning, we retire more or less unwillingly each night, and those two most commonplace reluctances enclose a pattern of activity which is best described by the poet who wearily protested,

> *I've done it all a thousand times,*
> *And all's to do again.*

The lives of most of us are monotonous. In the inimitable phrase of an outstanding contemporary satirist, the majority of people have but three unusual moments in their lives: when they are hatched, matched and dispatched. It follows, therefore, that a sincere Christian will need patience not only for the things that happen, but rather more especially for the things that don't happen. And let not any devout Catholic stenographer or insurance-salesman suspect for an instant that the life of a priest is really quite exciting. For the past twenty-five years I have been answering *Ora pro nobis* to the nightly Litany of the Saints.

The exercise is edifying, and, no doubt, beneficial. I grieve
to say it is not exhilarating. Unquestionably, Simeon must
have had dull days in the Temple. The point is that he
didn't stop going to the Temple. As a result, he was there
when his great happening did happen. His patience with
his monotony paid off.

Thirdly, kind reader and friend of Christ, you and I
must possess our souls in patience in this entire matter of
holiness. We touch here on a sharp but elusive point. Holiness, sanctity, perfection, solid moral goodness—call it
what you will, but call it by a name you *like*—is always
represented by spiritual guides as a goal of effort: we must
mend our ways, we must overcome ourselves, we must
walk the royal road of the cross, we must laboriously climb
the mountain of God. Now the first difficulty about such a
picture of the spiritual life is that it is perfectly true. Our
Savior Himself declared that we must be vigilant, that
we are to watch and pray (hard jobs, both), that the cross
must be shouldered daily. St. Paul has it that we are all
spiritual trackmen running in a race which is clearly no
hundred-yard dash. St. John practically said that we have
nothing to do but love one another, but what a large order
that is! So, unquestionably, the spiritual guides are correct
when they exhort us to pull in our belts and gird for the
battle and get up the spiritual steam.

But the second difficulty with this picture is that it is
quite incomplete; and the masters of the spirit, especially
really smart people like St. Augustine and St. Thomas the
Ox, tell us this, too. The struggle for holiness is not exactly
like the struggle to lose weight. If a brave trencherman
will actually, by brute force of will, confine his gastronom-

ical intake to one thousand calories a day, he will lose weight, and that is all there is to the matter, except that the brave trencherman will probably become a manic depressive. But if you or I decide at this moment that we are going to become saints, and genuinely and effectively proceed to take all the known and approved means to that end, that is *not* all there is to the matter. There is besides the whole mysterious, incalculable element of the utterly free, unfettered gift of God's grace.

Beyond the manifest justice, in view of God's free but real desire that all men be saved, of granting to each individual the degree and amount of actual grace abundantly sufficient for salvation, God our Lord lies under no particular contract toward any of us in the matter of grace. Read our Savior's parables and observe in the behavior of those kings and lords and masters of vineyards who represent almighty God what can only be called a certain free and almost furious independence of action. As our Lord makes perfectly clear, His Father is always fair, but His Father is always free. It follows that in the matter of holiness as distinct from the matter of salvation we will all become, with all our strivings, as perfect as God wishes us to be, and no more. Yet the odd and baffling part of the whole business—and, incidentally, the only really *practical* point —is that you and I absolutely must employ every effort, we must indeed pull in our belts and gird for the battle and turn on the spiritual steam, if we are to reach at all the degree of holiness which God our Lord has appointed for us. Some people, no doubt, would regard this as God's little joke on the human race. It isn't His little joke. It's His big love.

At any rate, anyone who is interested in genuine Christian moral goodness will have to be distinctly energetic, and, at the same time, distinctly patient. There are good souls who are forever taking their own spiritual measurements, like those more earthy folk who daily weigh themselves or the still more fascinating people who daily take their own temperature. As a glorious Christian—Chesterton—has pointed out, a really healthy man neither talks nor thinks about his health. A really spiritual man is, in a certain queer way, not interested in his spirit. He is interested in God. Next time you feel impelled to fetch out the yardstick and measure your own spiritual stature, suppose you measure God, instead. That will keep you happily occupied for some time to come.

Finally and briefly, we have to be patient about heaven. It is true, of course, that St. Paul ardently desired to pack off and to be with Christ; but there is no record, and not the slightest indication, that Paul in any sense dropped out of the race for the crown in order to catch his breath. In us, the pure desire to be quit of this world and to be with God forever is possibly not quite so pure as it was in Paul. By and large, this world is not a highly satisfactory place, and unfortunately, it cannot be said to improve on longer acquaintance. Still, it is the place of our probation, and although we may reasonably desire God's speedy and final approval, let us not hanker, even mentally, for any abridgement of the time of trial. Our going hence, like our coming hither, rests in quite safe hands. *In manus tuas, Domine, commendo spiritum meum: Into Thy hands, Lord, I commend my spirit.*

The nicest part of the story of old Simeon is, of course,

the happy ending. True, he had to be patient. True, he had to be patient for a long time. But he was not patient in vain. Let us be endlessly patient, you and I, in order that in the end we, too, may look into the face of Jesus.

"A voice was heard in Rama, lamentation and great mourning; it was Rachel weeping for her children . . ."

MATTHEW 2:18
JEREMIAS 31:15

V

THE HOLY INNOCENTS

One of the saddest events in our Lord's life took place soon after He was born, and the sad thing didn't happen to Him at all.

Matthew and Luke are the historians of our Savior's birth
and infancy, and their respective versions of the world's
most celebrated nativity complement and complete one
another perfectly. With stark brevity both Evangelists
record the earth-shaking and soul-shaking birth of the
Infant God as if completely conscious of the howling ab-
surdity of trying (as someone has said) to eff the ineffable.
At once Luke starts talking about the Shepherds and Matthew about the Magi. Luke proceeds to his trenchant
account of the circumcision and the first shedding of
Christ's blood. Matthew proceeds to tell us of a sadder
event, another shedding of blood, the first tragic happening
in the life of God made man. In order to explain the horrid
and incredible fact, Matthew tells us something of a man
whom history remembers, with colossal irony, under the
name of Herod the Great.

To give the devil his due, let us begin by conceding that
there was nothing small about Herod the Great. What he
did was often enough morally and shockingly wrong—

he had a pretty taste in murder—but it was never insignificant. His first and highest gift was political genius. Herod possessed to a really startling degree that unusual combination of vulpine sagacity, breath-taking boldness and unfathomable ruthlessness which makes the supreme politician. As one man seems predestined by the flexibility of his personality and even by the very neutrality and mobility of his countenance to be an actor, so Herod, by his whole background and interior equipment, seems predestined or perhaps doomed to have been a master-politician. By blood he was half-Arab, by profession and all seeming he was a Jew, in interior actuality he was a pagan, in taste he was Greek, in political sympathy (for he was a man who could excellently read handwriting on walls) he was Roman; in a sense of which St. Paul never dreamed, Herod the Great was all things to all men. Finally, Herod played in that prodigious luck which is really so much more than mere fortune. He hitched his political wagon to one meteoric star after another—Pompey, Caesar, Brutus, Antony—and, by one of the inscrutable mysteries of that most mysterious of all games, practical politics, his wagon rode higher and higher in the flaming wake of each falling star. The defeat of Antony and Cleopatra at Actium should have been the end of Herod, but it only roused him to the boldest and riskiest move of all. Without waiting for the fateful summons, he immediately sets sail for Rhodes, where Octavian Augustus is basking in the first flush of the victory which had put the world in his pocket.

Herod removes his diadem before he enters the audience room. He walks boldly towards Augustus and greets *him as a king greets his equal. He is no eastern potentate abased before the conqueror: he is bold, courageous, dignified. There are moments when truth is so unexpected that it carries all before it. This is one of them. Herod does not apologize for his friendship with the fallen Antony. He enlarges on it. He stresses his loyalty. He says that many a time he begged Antony to rid himself of Cleopatra, but nothing could save the man. He carried defeat in himself. Herod looks Augustus in the eyes. He has served Antony faithfully. He promises to serve Augustus as faithfully if he will accept him as the friend and ally of the Roman people. Augustus looks back into the clever, bold eyes of Herod and tells him to put on his diadem. So Herod wins again. After a triumphal progress with Augustus, he returns richer and more powerful. . . .**

Such was one side of the character of Herod the Great. The other side was pure savagery. He murdered three of his sons, Aristobulus, Alexander and Antipater; he executed his brother Pheroras and his sister Salome; of his favored wife's family he slew Hyrcanus, her grandfather, Alexandra, her mother, and Aristobulus, her brother. Miriamne herself, whom alone he seems to have loved, was the last to be butchered. He put to death forty-five members of the Jewish Sanhedrin who had opposed him, and in his last hideous sickness he left the incredible orders, never carried out, that a host of Jewish nobles whom he had summoned to Jericho should be slaughtered immediately upon his death, so that the whole country might effectively be thrown into mourning. It is small wonder, as a noted Scripture scholar has written, that the appalling deed to

* H. V. Morton: *In the Steps of the Master.*

which we now turn our attention, the slaughter of the Innocents, should have disappeared among all the infamies recorded of this dreadful man by secular history.

At some unknown time after the birth of our Lord in Bethlehem an impressive caravan came humping and thumping into Jerusalem. The travellers were grave and perhaps elderly men of that learned class who were known as Magi. The name *magus* originally designated a tribe in Persia, but had come to be applied to scholars who devoted themselves to Babylonian, that is, more or less nonreligious, learning: mathematics, natural science, astrology. Matthew is sufficiently vague about these pilgrims, although he is luminous on the nature of the pilgrimage which, after all, was his only point: we don't know the names of the Magi nor how many there were nor how in all the world they came upon the trail, if we may speak so, of the King of all the world. St. Matthew only remarks with a vague and sweeping gesture that the newcomers were from the East, thus leaving the industrious Scripture scholars room to move around in.

At any rate, the strangers to Jerusalem immediately began with calm seriousness to ask a question which ran through the bazaars like a flame and rocked the city like a bomb. No one seemed able or willing to answer the question, few were inclined even to discuss the question, and all were manifestly disturbed by the question as by a notable indelicacy. Very soon, however, an obsequious messenger presented himself to the Magi with an urgent invitation, which was very like a summons, from King Herod of this land of Judea. Serenely the Wise Men from the East followed the messenger to the royal palace, and then began a royal and intricate game of cat-and-mouse. It is impossible now to judge just how far the Wise Men bought, as we say today, what Herod was selling, but some days later the caravan from the East went swaying out of the Holy City on the road to the south. Cat Herod sat purring in his palace; the mice might be permitted to range thus far, for they were well within claw-reach, and the simpletons had not the faintest suspicion that they were being used to bait a larger trap. Herod was pleased with himself. Glutted with blood as he was, guile was beginning to appeal to him more strongly than gore.

Granted this man's character and fearful history, it is small wonder, really, that Herod simply exploded when, on a morning several days later, a panting courier burst in with the wild news that the Magi had not only slipped out of Bethlehem during the night, but were already well beyond the borders of Judea and the jurisdiction of King Herod. Herod's flaming wrath must have been something to witness as he realized that he, who had outwitted snake-eyed Octavian Augustus, the world's master, had been duped by a handful of soft-spoken, dreamy-eyed college professors. The cataclysmic fury of this horrible old butcher burst into such action as was strictly worthy of him. He screamed the ghastly orders; the detachment of indifferent, professional killers marched off to the south, and as the paranoiac rage of the king subsided, the pitiful wailing of women rose to smite the same Bethlehem skies that had poured out the now mystifying news of peace on earth. *A voice was heard in Rama, lamentation and great mourning; it was Rachel weeping for her chil-*

dren, and she would not be comforted, because none is left.[*]

Nineteen hundred years later I, one ordinary man who wears the uniform of Him who did *not* perish among the poor babies of Bethlehem, sit at a desk in a cheerful room and scribble words on paper. But I can hear the awful, desolate crying of the distracted mothers of so long ago; I can yet see the still little bodies, all slashed and smashed and sickening; I can picture one little Infant riding safely in His frightened Mother's arms into the secure asylum of Egypt. And I can only put into black words on white paper the honest, human thought that is in my heart. It is all so very strange. It *is* mysterious. The ways of this Christ Jesus are hard ways indeed.

Come, now, let me try. Surely the Holy Innocents, whose very name rings with a kind of careless gaiety, can do more for me than pose a paralyzing question. Surely these Infants who are so tenderly pictured in the liturgical hymn as playing before God's throne, baby-fashion, with the crowns and palms of martyrdom, surely they will as artlessly answer the very question they start. What *is* the explanation, so far as this brief world affords one, of all the Herods and slaughters and lifeless babies and heartbroken mothers that distract the pages of history and torment the days of life?

Any man who is normally honest and ordinarily thoughtful will sincerely maintain that he certainly doesn't expect to be exempted from the common burdens and sorrows of

[*] From the Old Testament Vol. II in the translation of Msgr. Ronald Knox, Copyright 1950, Sheed & Ward, Inc., New York.

all humanity. There are people, of course, who regard any
trouble that befalls them as uncommon and horrifying in
the extreme, simply because it befalls *them*, and I think I
have known a family who were perfectly willing to grant
that death must sooner or later pay his dark visit to every
house but theirs. Still, in general, people who think at all
will genuinely endorse for its truth, if not for its oily
glibness, the definitive observation of Hamlet's mother to
her son, and will apply it to many things besides death:

> *Thou know'st 'tis common. All that lives must die,*
> *Passing through nature to eternity* . . .

What frequently troubles us most sorely, however, is
not common, but uncommon evil, especially in the tor-
menting form of extreme suffering on the part of the innocent because of the criminal or careless or even casual
deeds of those who are far from innocent. When the hard-
working shopkeeper is shot down by a vicious young hood-
lum; when the beautiful little boy is mashed beyond recognition by the drunken driver who is never caught; when
the young husband and new father plunges in his flaming
plane to Korean earth because of the cold-blooded doings
of Malenkov and his crew; when the zealous priest must
leave the place he knows best and the work he does best
because of the poisonous tongues of some foul-minded
women; when the sweet young girl is hounded by a fierce
and devouring mother into a disastrous marriage in order
to keep her from going to the convent; when all these innocents are slaughtered, one way or another, by all these
Herods of both sexes, then indeed the mind of the help-
less spectator grows troubled, and his heart is torn with

an emotion which is all the sharper for being two-edged; for his very anguish seems a guilty thing. Why (we are forced to cry out in our pain) does God *allow* such evil? How can God stand quietly by while the vicious of this world, for their own dark ends, twist and tear the bodies and the hearts of the innocent? Doesn't God *care* what happens to the very people who are trying their best to believe in Him and love Him and serve Him?

We fold our hands and bow our heads and close our eyes, seeking in the silence and darkness of God's omnipresence for an answer; and there rises up before our imagination the Infant Christ sleeping quietly on His Mother's breast while, miles away, a baby, before the eyes of his screaming mother, is swung by a small ankle against a stone wall, and the soft, round head smashes like an eggshell.

Worse yet. Not only does God stand silently by while the innocent are racked and ravished by the guilty; God even seems in some way to gain, to profit by the awful suffering which He permits. We all know that no tiniest event can take place in the entire universe, that not a sparrow can perish nor a hair fall from a head nor a star wink its bright eye for a moment without God's willing it. We know likewise that the dark, ugly deeds of the evil in this world are not so much willed by God as permitted by Him. Yet isn't it true that every single event in the whole bewildering complexity of human history melts finally into a gigantic pattern which ultimately spells out the astonishing device, *The Glory of God*? Isn't it true that when the cruel telegram from the War Department was delivered to certain homes and the hoarse, unwonted shriek broke out and the torrent of tears began to flow—isn't it true that glory was being given to God in high heaven, though there be no peace on earth even for men of the best good will?

Once again we fold our hands and bow our heads and close our eyes in God's presence; and now there rises before the mind's eye another familiar picture: we see patient Joseph plodding along, leading along the road to the haven of Egypt the donkey upon which Mary rides, she holding tight to her breast the Treasure in her arms. They are over the border now, they are quite safe. The little Christ sleeps in all peace, apparently. But what of those other Bethlehem babies who now sleep the last sleep of all, what of the poor mothers whose arms, unlike Mary's, are empty, and whose hearts are all torn and raw? It does seem, does it not, that God actually gains by the agony of the creatures He has made?

If we are not to be trapped by this persuasive and wholly human way of thinking, we must resolutely direct our thoughts to several less vivid, less emotional, but far more factual considerations. However strange the plea may sound, let us creatures try to be fair to our Creator in this matter of suffering. Let us try to be as fair as the Holy Innocents and their mothers would now want us to be.

To begin with, we cannot afford to forget that human existence is now being governed, in the providence of God, by an alternative over-all plan. The unfailing temptation to read into the word *alternative* the perfectly gratuitous meaning of *inferior* or *second-rate* must be stubbornly resisted; for God's present dispensation for humanity is thunderingly neither inferior nor second-rate, and yet it is unquestionably an alternative plan. Always granted that it is as confusing for us to talk about what

God does as it is to talk about what God is, we may yet recall that since Adam and Eve were created, a) in a state of original justice or sanctifying grace and, b) emphatically possessed of unhampered and authentic free will, there must have existed in what we will desperately call God's original designs both a plan or dispensation based on the supposition of man's perfect obedience to the initial imperative, and an alternative plan or dispensation based on the supposition, subsequently and sadly verified in fact, of the original disobedience. Now it cannot be that God *preferred* that Adam and Eve sin; His clear imperative, armed with deadly sanction, can only mean that God preferred that the first human beings obey Him. It follows, therefore, that God's *preferred* plan for mankind is not in operation at all. God our Lord never did desire death, never did seek for sickness, never did intend tears. In the oddly obscure yet blazing light of God's gigantic and joyous original cosmic design we can perceive with certainty that in a very real sense God has nothing to do with suffering at all. Moral evil, with its inevitable camp-follower, suffering, is *our* contribution to the sum of existent reality. When we go crying to Supreme Goodness about human pain, God our Lord would be perfectly justified—though He would never be so churlish—in answering us thus: "Suffering? Don't ask me about it. Ask the man who in every sense owns it." The problem of evil is in a very strict sense humanity's baby. We may not like the problem, but we have got to live with it. It is indeed the fruit of our womb and the work of our hands.

Besides, it is monstrous to read into the valid concept of the glory of God as the final end of all reality the merely human idea of a sort of relish or enjoyment such as we would derive from any petty glory that might come to us. That external glory of God which alone finally warrants the existence of a wind or a weed or a whale is as pure and as innocent, so to speak, as a reflection in a mirror; for it is nothing else; it is nothing but the limitless gorgeousness of God Himself reflected in the vast pool of creation. If it could be remotely true that God our Lord, like the fierce and sensual and wholly anthropomorphic gods of Homer, derives some perverse satisfaction, as we understand the term, from the awful spectacle of human agony, then Christ Jesus, the God-man, made a very strange image of His Father as He healed the sick and consoled the afflicted and wept for dead Lazarus and pitied the multitudes who were as sheep without a shepherd and said to the widow of Naim, *Don't cry.* Yet our Lord did say to Philip at the Last Supper, *Whoever has seen Me, has seen the Father.*

No, God our Father does not enjoy our suffering. He does not drink our tears any more than He drank the blood of the ancient sacrifices of the Old Law. God does two things about our human anguish: He permits it; and, if we will allow Him, He transmutes and transforms and transfigures it. Human agony serves God well only in the sense in which it will serve us well: if we will make it a new scarlet and flaming bond that clasps and clamps us in tighter and mightier love to God Himself as distinct and separate from all God's gifts. It cannot be too often repeated that human suffering is meaningless, it is no more than a racking of limbs and a screaming tension of nerves and a shredding of a muscle called the heart, it is no more in a mother than it is in a mare, no more in a sweetheart than it is in a swallow, no more in a baby than it is in a baboon, it is indeed nothing but a curse and a nightmare and a life-long lunacy—unless and until I bow my head and bend my knees and force from my tight lips and cringing heart the terrible and transforming prayer: *Not my will, but Thine be done.*

There is a further and compelling consideration. We always think of God as witnessing our agony. It is strange that we do not much more often think of the far more pertinent and heartrending truth: that God shared our agony. Perhaps, without rashness, we may set it down as a fact that Christians generally do not give sufficient thought to the Passion of Christ. One of the really urgent reasons for the practice of mental prayer—which simply means thinking (for example) about Christ being scourged, and talking to Him as He is scourged, rather than stringing together another collection of wandering Our Fathers and Hail Marys—is the crying need of good people for a deeper understanding of the last eighteen hours of our Savior's mortal life. Any Christian can tell you that Christ died to save us, and in that utterly primitive sense everyone understands the Passion. But why need the Passion of Christ have been precisely as it was? What specific reason must there be for a writhing agony in a Garden, for a betrayal with—of all things!—a kiss, for whipping and thorns and slugging and kicks and spit in the face and such an unearthly, frightening cry as *My God, my God, why hast thou forsaken Me?*

It is, in very truth, only when we, who endorse the doctrines of Christ Jesus, begin to ask in prayer this piercing question, that we begin to discover and imbibe anything like the Christ-attitude on the subject of suffering. How anyone can think for a moment of God our Lord as impassively looking on at the spectacle of human anguish when, in fact, God-made-man has actually drained to the last revolting drop the bitter cup of every possible type of human torment—that is a question which will look long for a reasonable and fair-minded answer. It is not on Thabor in the white splendor of the Transfiguration, nor when He is calming a storm at sea, or calling the dead from their graves that Jesus is most truly one of us. But there was more than miracles and magnificence to the mortal life of God's own Son. The whips raised welts on His back as they would on ours; to be framed and cheated and slandered and sold out by His friend of years stung and burned His Heart as it would ours; the nails tore His hand and feet as they would mine or yours, and when at last He hung between heaven and earth, lost to His Mother and abandoned by His Father, His piteous cry of loneliness welled up from a Heart as broken as yours or mine would have been. God did so terribly become one of us: in the cradle; on the cross; in the grave. And to this God we creep, muttering and snivelling and wailing about our woes, but always warily averting our look from the very One to whom we speak, lest perchance we see the thorns upon His head and the gaping holes in His hands and the awful, unfathomable look in His eyes. We may be sure of it: who is most sorely touched by the problem of pain is not touched at all by the sharpest pain of all—the pain of Christ.

Yes, the Holy Innocents perished while the Infant Savior escaped. Yes, Mary probably slept on the night when there was no sleep for the mothers of Bethlehem. Yes, Christ and His Mother were saved from all that horror. They were saved indeed: He for a cross, she to stand beside it.

"They, leaving their father Zebedee in the boat with the hired men, turned aside after Him."

MARK 1:20

VI

ZEBEDEE

Not much has been written about the father of James and John, because there isn't much to write. There is *something*, though; and it should be written in very large letters.

Some Biblical names are either so elusive or so forbidding or so unpronounceable that we tend not only to forget them easily but forget them with a sort of vague relief. Amaleg and Nebuchodonosor and Baal and Barsabas are all undoubtedly memorable, but they come close to being, in the exact sense, unspeakable. Perhaps that is the first reason, however trivial and accidental it may be, for a certain affection I have always felt for a man who is barely mentioned in the Gospels, the father of the Apostles James and John. Zebedee is a name worth having, and well worth remembering if you don't have it. The name zips like the flight of a bird and sings like the bird itself. The distribution of vowels and consonants is perfect; and if any villainous philologist should carp about a certain monotony of vowels in this kingly appellation, the fellow must simply be referred to the musical beauty of a name like Barbara.

Regrettably, we haven't much more about Zebedee than his name. John and James are occasionally mentioned with their patronymic, but we recall that our Savior, in His

usual quiet and casual way, even changed *that* by re-
naming these frankly favored brothers the Boanerges, that
is, the Sons of Thunder. At any rate, Zebedee actually
appears in the Gospel story just once. He says nothing,
and, in a most exact sense, he does nothing, although, at
the moment we catch sight of him, he is patching a torn
net. Yet that single appearance in the Gospel narrative is
not without significance. Let us think about it.

We know precisely four facts about this man Zebedee.
He was a fisherman; he had an amazing wife; he was the
father of two grown boys; and—but let the last fact wait.
For it is the central fact. It is the whole point. It is the
story of Zebedee.

Sometime around what we would call January of the
year 27 A.D., John Barzebedee was apparently taking a
little vacation from the fish business. At the time, he was
not in Galilee at all, where his family lived and worked,
but down south in Judea, where he had become involved
in an unusual religious movement headed by another John,
a striking, gaunt figure who had burst like a portent out of
the wilderness. John of Galilee had become a disciple—we
cannot judge in what degree of permanence—of John of
Judea, when suddenly there appeared on the banks of the
Jordan a third Person who clearly was not anyone's disciple
and who, indeed, seemed not quite like anyone else in the
world. The effect of this newcomer on the Baptist was
notable. Formerly, the Baptist, for all his fierce concentration on his work, had had the somewhat abstracted air
of a man listening for something or waiting for someone.
Now, after a short, sharp exchange with the Stranger, John
of Judea had clearly heard to his satisfaction what he had

been listening for, and he promptly proceeded to advertise to his own followers that here finally was the Someone he had been waiting for. In particular, when the impressive Stranger, on the afternoon after His baptism, walked quietly past the Baptist and a pair of his followers, the Baptist had pointed to Him and said, in an odd formula, *Look, there is the Lamb of God.* A moment later the two disciples parted from John with a finality of which they did not dream, and went trailing like sheep after this Lamb of God. The names of the two were John, the son of Zebedee, and Andrew, brother to another Galilean fisherman named Simon. Many years later, when he was a very old man, this John the Evangelist remembered and set down in his Gospel the very hour of the day at which he had begun to follow Christ Jesus: it was at four o'clock in the afternoon, he says simply.

It is difficult to determine in exactly what sense John and Andrew and Peter and the others then became disciples of Christ. Possibly they undertook to be what we would call part-time disciples, for when we meet them subsequently in their native Galilee, they are back at work trying to earn a living—lean enough, apparently—as fishermen on that Lake of Genesareth which figures so largely in the life of our Lord. On the eastern shore of this lake, a year or less after the first meeting between Christ and these simple, hearty friends of His, a further event took place which established much more definitively the relationship between them.

Early on a certain morning our Savior had come down to the lake shore, where a goodly number of people could always be found, to start another day of work on the movement, or, as He always called it, the kingdom which He had come to found. The crowd on this particular morning proved to be unusually large and unusually eager, and, after the manner of crowds everywhere and always, they soon had pushed their hero of the moment to the brink of something—in this case, the lake. Incidentally, a never-ending subject for the meditation of the thoughtful is the way in which the Son of God permitted Himself to be pushed around by people in the literal as well as the metaphorical sense of the phrase. Christ has more sympathy for subway riders and bus commuters than they might expect. On the present occasion our good Lord was as patient and cheerful and resourceful as ever. If His too-eager flock would not allow Him standing-room by the lake, faithful Simon Peter could be depended upon to give Him a seat on it. A few minutes later, Christ our Lord, in one of the most charming of the Gospel scenes, was seated at His ease in Peter's fishing boat some little distance from shore, while the lake which He had made served its Creator well as a watery barrier against hyperenthusiasts. Under such delightful circumstances our Savior began energetically to break the bread of life to the hungry, humble folk who needed Him so badly and whom He loved so well.

Never Christ to accept a kind service without putting His gratitude into word or act. When He had finished His instruction and the crowd began to melt away, our Savior turned cheerfully to Peter and said, equivalently, "And now let us go fishing." Inwardly poor Peter groaned. Chief among the few things he really knew well stood the business of fishing in the Lake of Galilee. He knew, as he knew his own name, that Galilean fish were simply not caught during the day. At the moment, Peter knew, in addition, that in their present wilful mood Galilean fish were not even being caught at night; his heavy eyelids (and I have always wondered if Peter slept during our Lord's sermon that morning) and aching arms were strong reminders of the wasted night he and his fellows had just put in. Peter couldn't repress a mild protest, but with something like heroic generosity he agreed to humor this beloved Master of his who had probably enjoyed a sound night's rest. The sail was run up, and the skiff gently heeled over and made for deep water. Peter and the others were probably painfully polite as they wearily ran the dragnet over the side of the boat; but in a few minutes they had clean forgotten both politeness and weariness as they tugged and heaved and shouted for another boat and crew and generally worked themselves into that special hysteria of fishermen who are afraid that the big ones will get away. Later, when boats and crew and splendid catch were all safely ashore, and honest Peter had fallen on his knees before his Master in wonder and love, he and his brother Andrew had heard from the lips of Christ the quiet, shining declaration that made the turning point in their lives: *From now on you will be fishers of men.*

Our Savior turned away and walked along the lake shore with the air of one who has something further to do. He stopped where the nets of Zebedee and company were already spread out to the sun while Zebedee, John, James and the hired men carefully checked for tears and breaks that the big catch might have made. In the same quiet voice Jesus addressed a few words to John and James. Everyone stopped working. The two young men looked at

Christ, they looked at one another, they looked long and last at their father. If any word was spoken it is not recorded. John and James picked up the cloaks which they had laid aside while they worked, and walked over to where Peter and Andrew stood beside the Master. The little company moved slowly away. We last see Zebedee standing there among the hired men (as Mark explicitly says) holding a strand of net in his hands and watching his sons and his future walk away from him.

That is the story of the man Zebedee. That is the whole story. And it is tremendous. He gave his sons to Christ.

No one, surely, will understand as a silly boast the obvious statement that certain common words hold a highly special meaning for people who happen to be genuine Catholics: such words, for example, as benediction and penance and host and fish. Definitely among these specialized expressions stands the word *vocation*. Vocation is worth talking and thinking about. For any Catholic parents vocation may cease at any time to be a mere word, and begin to be, according to the nature of the parents, a wonder or a worry. Shall we talk about vocation and parents?

It had better be insisted from the outset that there is one aspect of this vocation business which cannot be made clear to parents for the simple reason that it is not clear to anybody, least of all to those who have a vocation. The question, Why does God our Lord call *this* boy or *this* girl to His service?—is flatly unanswerable. People are not summoned to the religious or priestly life for their looks or their money or their brains or even, in any profound sense, for their character. The utterly unpredictable choice of God, which at times seems positively flighty, cuts full across all human classifications and categories. A boy will be raised in the lap of luxury, and then fuss and fidget until he finds himself in a Trappist monastery. A girl grows up in a vicious slums where purity is a joke, and presents herself, aged seventeen, shining and serene and spotless at the convent gate. Lads who quake and shake if they must stand up to speak three sentences to three people in a high-school public speaking class finally mutter an indistinguishable word of thanks as they are handed a diploma, and then hurry off to the Order of Preachers. And young men who are totally without either guile or gall suddenly begin to insist that they want to become Jesuits.

There is no explaining these strange goings-on, because there is no understanding them. *The Wind breathes where it will,* said our Savior to learned Nicodemus, and whether He was talking about that mighty pentecostal breath which is the Holy Spirit or merely about the wild west wind, the remark holds for One as for the other. In the matter of vocation God's selection is so arbitrary as to be at times incredible, and so astonishing as to seem at times wholly unreasonable. Hopeless, therefore, is any attempt to explain to parents why God wants their boy or their girl. I don't *know* why. I still don't know why God called the youngest son of my own mother and father. It was divinely optimistic and, so to say, unselfish of God, as I see with more luminous clarity each passing hour. Happily, though, I did not question the fact; and neither—God rest their great souls!—did my mother and father.

About another aspect of religious vocation there is no

mystery at all. The clerical or monastic or convent habit or garb may not look like much, but it is in fact an extremely costly vesture. As someone or other has shrewdly pointed out, there is this striking initial difference between marriage and religious life: marriage begins at a peak of happiness, and then commonly (saving only the case of the present married reader) tends to grow more difficult; religious life begins at a peak of difficulty and frequently, if anyone wants to know, at a positive nadir of human satisfaction, and tends to grow happier as time passes. Consequently, the process of following out a vocation is apt to involve considerable initial pain for both the called youth and the challenged and maybe chilled parents.

No doubt it is at least conceivable that a fairly normal young person might choose a life of poverty, chastity or obedience in a passing mood of romantic infatuation, but the possibility is flatly unlikely; far and away more unlikely than the possibility of mere passing infatuation in those adolescent affairs of the heart which certain retarded parents take pains to foster and encourage. I should like to declare most solemnly, certain that priests and Sisters everywhere will heartily join me in a positive chorus of unanimity, that in nine cases out of ten the young person reacts to the first authentic stirrings of vocation with uneasiness, apprehension, alarm and with no end of reluctance, precisely because he is *not* infatuated with religious life.

In the conflicts which arise on this subject of vocation no one seems to observe that the boy or girl is not embarking on a lark or a honeymoon or a picnic or a holiday cruise, but is consciously making a *sacrifice*, and making it as normal people make any sacrifice, with real pain. Now don't we teach children from their most tender years that it is a noble and generous thing to make a personal sacrifice in a good cause? If this is not what we teach under the heading of patriotism, family devotion, love of neighbor and even common decency, then what in the world *do* we teach in such worthy connections? Why, then, when there is question of a generous young person making the supreme sacrifice for the supreme cause of the Supreme Being, why do we suddenly begin to suggest with much assurance that here is no question of a noble sacrifice at all, but only of silly infatuation? Why is a boy a hero if he risks his life to save his country from being invaded or his sister from being insulted or his dog Fido from being drowned, and why is a girl a heroine if she nurses the contagious sick or marries a blind soldier or snatches a canary from a ferocious cat; and yet both of them merely foolish and even selfish and unfeeling if they only want to give their lives to God? For my single self, I am definitely weary of hearing how hard it is for mother and father when Johnny or Janie leaves home for religion. I want to hear more about how hard it is for Johnny and Janie. I happen to know something about *that*.

That vocation involves real sacrifice and therefore real pain on the part of devoted parents, no one will trouble to deny. As has already been remarked, we don't know why God calls your boy or your girl. We don't know, either, why it was the boy next door who was killed in Korea last year.

As a matter of fact, normal Catholic parents are as normally generous in this delicate matter as they are in lesser connections. Indeed, Catholic parents invariably rejoice over a vocation in the house as they would over a new baby in the house, rightly believing that a vocation is an honor to the whole family and a sure mark of God's particular love for this particular mother and father. But now we come to the most mysterious of all the mysteries that cluster around the very central mystery of religious vocation, and it is this. Why do so many contemporary Catholic parents regard it as a joy and an honor if their son wants to become a priest, and regard it as an affliction and a reproach if their daughter wants to become a nun? If anyone has any sort of reasonable answer to this most vexing question, I earnestly wish I could have a long talk with him. In the most despairing manner, the present writer will now attempt a feeble analysis of this really infuriating problem. There may be some who do not concede the fact, who do not believe that the matter stands as we have stated it. I envy them their happy and innocent frame of mind.

Let us first examine the objections which parents raise and the reasons which they allege when they oppose a daughter's desire to enter the convent. This entire discussion will hold in due proportion when parents object to a son becoming a priest or a Brother; but this alternative phenomenon is so rare as to be negligible. Which point is interesting in itself. Does anyone else think, as this person does, that, in general, parents have much less success in attempting to run the lives of their sons than they do in trying to run the lives of their daughters?

At any rate, there is no question about what commonly happens first, when daughter Susan suddenly announces with heigh-ho and hey-nonny-nonny that she is off to the convent come September a year. The family reaction, after the first merry laughter and flat disbelief, is instant and unanimous: Susan is too young for any such thing.

At this point the afflicted writer chews on his pencil (for thus primitively does he write) like a two-year-old colt at a bit. The temptation to embark on an entirely distinct essay entitled *For Sweet Heaven's Sake, When Do Young People Grow Up?* is violent, but must be resisted in the interests of orderly discussion, the reader's patience and the writer's nervous system. We will only quote a single remark of one of the truly penetrating writers of our century, the Abbé Ernest Dimnet, when he is speaking of the men of all the pre-scientific periods: "A man of twenty-six was a man and not a boy, as we foolishly imagine and openly say, to the detriment of the race by the diffusion of a dangerous illusion." In our present instance, Susan may not be twenty-six; but she isn't six, either.

However, Susan at seventeen or eighteen is held to be much too young to enter the convent; so Susan is held. We wish now to invoke the familiar and veritable distinction which the philosophers and lawyers express through the terms *de jure* and *de facto*. *De jure* or as a matter of right and justice, Susan *ought* not to be too young to take the first definite step which would lead to an irrevocable decision. *De facto* or as a matter of brute, plain fact, maybe Susan *is* too young for any such step. Since girls seem nowadays to be raised in really protective custody, not in the sound old sense of being shielded from evil, but in the broader, modern sense of being shielded from responsibility, practical household work and effective decisions of any sort, it may jolly well be that Susan is indeed too young for the commitment represented by entrance into the convent. Very well.

Let us not stop, however, in the very middle of the argument. Let us not rest content with drawing such a limited conclusion from such rich and promising premises. The real truth which both Susan and her parents must face at peril of dishonesty, quackery, deceit and double-dealing with almighty God, is this: if Susan is too young for anything as decisive as entering the convent, then she is exactly that; she is too young for *anything else* which is a first step in the direction of an irrevocable decision. Not only, in this case, is Susan too young for marriage, which is obvious; she is also too young for anything like an engagement, and likewise much too young for what is termed *going steady*. Isn't going steady the first manifest step in the direction of an irrevocable decision? Susan is also too young for commitment to any career. If she inclines to be a nurse, a secretary or a lady channel-swimmer, the whole thing must be kept entirely tentative, any plan must simply be taken under cautious advisement; and if Susan is going to college (a perilous step) or going into a business office (a fate worse than death), she must be wary of anything so final as choosing a particular course of studies or giving the boss any impression that she intends to stay on in her job. In other words, it is patently unfair and manifestly partial to say that Susan is too young to enter the convent. Susan is too simply too young; too young for anything; certainly too young for anything high or fine or brave.

Very well, then, Susan is too young for the convent. Let her go to college and take any course that appeals to mother or let her get a job in some office that father will recommend. We have only one final suggestion for Susan, and it seems to us that the girl ought to be amenable to our counsel, since, if we do not love her more than her parents do, we obviously respect her a great deal more. Susan should draw up a document, a document as formal and official as a contract in law. (Any priest or Sister will be glad to help Sue with the job.) The document will state that at the conclusion of two calendar years after graduation from high school, Susan will be utterly and entirely free to make whatever choice she wishes with regard to her future; and that Susan's parents now solemnly promise such freedom in return for Susan's generous surrender to them of the next two years of her life. Susan should get her parents to sign this document. Sign it, mind you, nothing less; and preferably before witnesses. Let Susan not take any verbal promise or spoken guarantee, for if she does, she will be hoodwinked. I know, because I know Susan's parents. I have met them a dozen times. On this subject they are cheats and liars.

The second objection of parents to the following of a vocation is that the boy or girl is under undue influence from the Sisters and priests. This is an interesting contention, if only because it is sometimes true. There are indeed religious, more zealous than wise, who love to take over some of the functions of the Holy Spirit, and who take it upon themselves to do the work in the Church that a recruiting sergeant does in the army. If anyone cares, the present writer has discussed or maybe attacked this little tendency in a previous volume of wandering reflection.* If there be any reasonable suspicion of such ill-advised recruiting in a particular case, parents will do well to urge a moratorium on the whole matter, during which the young person should be removed from the recruiter's sphere of influence. In all fairness, however, we might pause to wonder just how common this vocational high-pressuring really is. The writer can do no more than report his actual experience of this business. He has met it. He has not met it often. He has never met it in the more *intelligent* priests and Sisters; and they really do constitute a thumping majority in the ranks of the clergy and religious.

Finally, parents resist a vocation in a child because, as they say, religious life, especially for a Sister, is simply too hard. A girl in the convent is fearfully cooped up, she is deprived of normal social development, she must live without the soft, *nice* things that women so love, she must work endlessly and to exhaustion. All of which is true. And anyone with half an eye can see in nuns the sad, disastrous effects of such a mode of existence. Cooped up as she is, the young girl must drag along without the cultural influence of the daily newspaper, *Collier's* and *Vogue*; she loses the humanizing effect of daily trips in the subway or commuter's bus; she must forego the soft lights and the gentle laughter of the local Stork Club or a neighborhood bar. Deprived as she is of normal social evolution, she develops that harshness, that loud brassiness, that sharp angularity which we have all observed in nuns as contrasted with the soft-spoken and polished women of the world. Since she must live without the *nice* things of life,

* *Most Worthy of All Praise,* Declan X. McMullen Co., 1945.

her naturally fine feminine taste degenerates into the gross crudity so noticeable among Sisters. Worked and overworked, she grows old before her time, and the old antic, death, is commonly grinning over her stooped shoulders before she reaches eighty or eighty-five. Ain't it awful?

Presuming on the patience of whatever long-suffering readers remain at this point, we beg leave to suggest the real as opposed to the alleged reasons for parental opposition to vocation. These real reasons are two: lack of faith and lack of love.

Catholic parents who would welcome a vocation for their son but oppose a vocation for their daughter may be certain that their whole view of vocation is merely natural, and not supernatural at all. They are delighted to have a priest in the family simply and purely because the priest means prestige. They would dread having a nun in the family, because someone is bound to say sooner or later that the girl went to the convent when she couldn't get a man. With the priest goes notice, applause, a certain amount of the human and much-loved spotlight. When Sister comes home she brings nothing much with her, really: only Christ in her clear eyes and quiet words and quick, joyous smile. Of course it doesn't amount to anything to have a Sister of Mercy or Charity or Notre Dame —such lovely names!—in the family. The reader must not mind if I sound a little wistful. We just didn't happen to have a Sister in our house.

The other real reason why parents sometimes hold out against a vocation is lack of love. Not only do such people lack supernatural love of God; they lack natural love of their own children. Parental love is pure only when it is purged of all possessiveness. Obviously, the love of a certain number of contemporary parents for their children is not very pure. It is a strange and sad fact that for some extremely selfish human beings one life is not enough. For them, children represent, above everything else, a golden opportunity to live again, to live vicariously, voraciously and voluptuously. For such parents sons and daughters are, in the psychological order, pretty much what a living animal is to the vampire-bat in the physical order: a meal-ticket. The children are the hollow men. The parents are the real McCoy.

Zebedee! Zebedee, old man, now no longer standing by the shore, the net-strands between your fingers and that unfathomable look in your eyes! Zebedee, now sitting contented and replete at the banquet-board of the Beatific Vision! Do you remember the sunny day when you nodded your old head ever so slightly, and your two boys walked off with Christ Jesus? Yes, you remember. And don't think for a moment that you are pulling any wool over our twentieth-century eyes. You were a fox, and you know it. You could have held on to your two lads, and with them gone down into that sea of oblivion which is so much deeper and blacker than the Sea of Galilee. Like all the other father-fishermen of that lake shore, you could have possessed everlasting forgotten-ness, you could have been unknown to all the ages, if you had only shaken your head. You were smart, Zebedee. You will be known when kings are forgotten, you, the proud father of *two* Apostles.

And Jesus went into Peter's house, and found his wife's mother lying sick
there with a fever.

MATTHEW 8:14

VII

SIMON PETER'S MOTHER-IN-LAW

It practically amounts to a comic story that one of the Gospel characters of
whom we almost never speak is—of all things—a mother-in-law!

Early in the public life of our Lord and Savior, the Word Incarnate, there occurred that sunny period which is sometimes called, in the whole pattern of Christ's life, the Galilean idyll. Let us speak of it.

It seems to have been about January of the year 27 A.D., when our Lord, according to a recommended chronology, was just past His thirty-first birthday, that the Son of Man bade farewell to His beloved Mother at Nazareth and struck south for the district around Jordan, in Judea, where John, called the Baptist, was thundering to all Israel the message of repentance in preparation for the imminent coming of Messias. With none but that John heeding and knowing, Messias humbly went through the ceremony of John's baptism, and immediately withdrew from all human society in order to perform His allotted share of bodily penance for our learning and in order to serve notice, *vis-à-vis*, to the baleful Enemy that the battle for mankind was now joined.

Early in March the Son of Mary, somewhat pale and a

bit gaunt, yet drawn utterly fine in the full, trim vigor of
His young manhood, reappeared on Jordan's banks. John,
alert and watching, knew well it was the hour. With one
final glance about him at the religious movement he had
built and at the devoted disciples he had trained, the Baptist pointed, pronounced his now consecrated formula of
self-obliteration—*Behold the Lamb of God!*—and stepped
back into the lengthening shadows of an obscurity which
would only be lit up by the blade-flash that would end his
life. On the following day our Savior, accompanied by His
five brand-new disciples, took the road that led north to
His native Galilee.

That first return to the north was brief, however. The
trip seems to have had only the purpose of setting up at
busy Capharnaum, on the western shore of Lake Genesareth, what we would call, in our awful jargon, operational
headquarters, though it is possible that our Savior especially wished to see His Mother at this juncture, for it was
on this visit that the first miracle, the wedding-wonder at
Cana, was performed. But our Lord and the disciples, like
the good Jews they were, returned at once to Judea and
Jerusalem for the great festival of the Passover. Promptly
Christ launched His Judean ministry with the sensational
and significant cleansing of the Temple. A storm of hos-
tility broke out, of course, and our Lord withdrew to a
district north of Jerusalem, where, with His disciples, He
began to exercise a quiet, systematic ministry modeled
after the Baptist's. Apparently this odd sort of interim
activity lasted only some six weeks; one gets the impression that our Savior was waiting for something. Suddenly
the soldiers of *that fox*, wily Herod Antipas, swooped down

upon the Jordan and arrested John Baptist. Immediately our Lord and His people left Judea for Galilee.

The Galilean idyll followed. Beginning with the striking cure of the son of an official personage, a cure all the more striking because it was worked *in absentia,* and ending with the official choice of the twelve Apostles and the Sermon on the Mount, this unique period in the life of Christ extended from the late spring through high summer of the year 27 A.D. It is a time of abounding miracles and mounting popularity, a time of insignificant opposition and ever-swelling success. An idyll it was, a sort of Arcadian interlude for our Lord which would never be repeated. There might be a terrible truth in saying that Jesus Christ was the Man of the Year for a fair section of Jewry in 27 A.D. He was that, but that was all. Couple of years later the Man of the Year seems to have been a ringer from Rome: Pontius Pilate.

During the Galilean idyll miracles were so plentiful that a number of them are listed by the Evangelists almost in catalogue fashion and with an absent-minded lack of detail that is exasperating. In Capharnaum, for example, our Savior and the disciples returned one Saturday morning from the synagogue, where Christ had clashed, briefly but fiercely, with a man suffering from demoniac possession, and had sternly expelled the vicious trespasser of a human personality. They entered the home of Simon Peter, no doubt for their midday meal, only to find Peter's mother-in-law prostrate with a burning fever. Our Savior took the lady by the hand, the fever immediately left her, and she rose to get the dinner ready. Such is the entire story. In a moment the Evangelists are off on another narrative, blandly and happily unconscious of the time-bomb they have cheerfully left behind them. The eyes of the centuries have focused—some in shock, some in gloating triumph, all in some surprise—on this relatively insignificant miracle. The miracle may be relatively unimportant, but the relative in the miracle is very far from unimportant. She represents what newsmen call a scoop, and a scoop of magnitude. So Simon Peter had a mother-in-law! So the first pope was a married man!

Stop the presses. . . .

Among a certain few subjects which, first, profoundly interest almost everybody and which, secondly, make a lot of people finally so mad that they could and frequently do want to fight, the matter of celibacy, and particularly voluntary celibacy, and most especially the celibacy of the Catholic clergy, holds a place which, by an understatement, might be termed *prominent.*

Celibacy, or the state of what is sometimes called single blessedness, has never been overwhelmingly popular in the human family, and that last accidental phrase becomes at once significant in such a context. There is not the slightest likelihood, as Mr. Shaw remarked long ago, that marriage as an institution will ever decline in popularity. Most men have not particularly speculated on the whole matter, any more than they speculate about the human business of eating. They simply eat, and they simply marry, and there's an end. Those who have speculated or philosophized on the subject of marriage have come up with an agreement so universal that no more attention need be paid to the few cranks who say that people should not marry than we pay to the very few lunatics who say that people should not wear clothes. So it has been most generally agreed, 1) that marriage is natural, 2) that marriage is beneficial, 3) that marriage is necessary.

It is instantly clear that no possible argument could be stirred up on either of the first two propositions listed. When we come, however, to the unadorned assertion that marriage is necessary, we are obliged to pause and wonder a little, and that, be it noted, for a reason that has nothing whatever to do with religion. The fact is that some people do not marry. Now whether that is a good fact or a bad fact, a strictly inevitable fact or a fact that results from free volition, it remains a fact. In addition, those unmarried people do not seem to slit either their throats or their wrists in great numbers, they do not in droves leap from bridges and windows, they do not all finally seal up their lonely kitchens and turn on the friendly gas. People do indeed do all these things, but it has never been demonstrated or even especially suggested that such folk are invariably spinsters or bachelors. If anything—but let us not attempt to prove too much. It is only necessary, in the light of these simple and obvious actualities, to wonder exactly what we mean when we contend (if we do) that marriage is a strict necessity.

The further point is indeed the religious one; but let it be observed from the outset that this complication of the matter is by no manner of means specifically Catholic or even specifically Christian.

Our good friends the professional anthropologists are the first to assure us, even when they themselves are not sympathetic to the idea, that people everywhere and always have believed in and worshipped some sort of god. Now the practical process of worshipping any god and most of all the true God has always posed a slight problem for human beings: just how do you worship a god? Guided by a sure and deep instinct, people have realized that there must be something more to religion (for that is what the worship of God is) than the periodic mouthing of formulae; they saw clearly that a man ought to *do* something for his god, even if that meant, as it sometimes did, *not* doing something in honor of the god. So men prostrated their bodies before idols, they sang and danced and, in the jollier religions, got drunk; they taxed their physical endurance in all sorts of ways, they fasted and sat immobile for hours and scourged themselves and sprinkled ashes on their heads. Above all, men struggled and strove against the very conditions of their creaturehood in order to make a true and precious gift to their god: that is, they offered some kind of visible sacrifice, as every religion did before the advent of Protestantism. All this is a clear matter of human record.

It is equally clear in the human record which is history that men have always and invariably believed that one distinct manner of worshipping a god was to bind themselves to absolute or periodic chastity in honor of that god. As everyone knows, the ancient Greeks and Romans were not particularly pious or especially edifying people, yet both paid lip-service and sometimes considerably more to the ideal of virginity as embodied in the cult of Artemis and/or Diana. The Romans, moreover, were quite strict about their vestal virgins and tended to be impatient when the virgins turned out not to be virgins. We read also that requirements, at times most rigid, in the matter of chastity have existed in many primitive tribes when it came to the matter of setting aside chosen people as special servants of the god, or, in other words, of setting up a priesthood.

We will not here attempt an inquiry into the significant question of *why* men have so regularly thought of chastity as a way to serve and please a god, for we are now concerned solely with the indubitable historical fact. We are only interested to suggest that if anyone objects to Catholicism because it has a celibate clergy, the objector must continue to object to a great number of religions apart from Catholicism, among them a considerable sector of modern Anglicanism or Episcopalianism.

It is perfectly true, of course, to assert that the Catholic clergy was not always celibate, for, as far as can now be discovered, the earliest Christian priesthood was neither *de facto* nor *de jure* celibate: neither as a matter of fact nor as a matter of obligation. St. Paul's famous directive to Timothy and to Titus, that a bishop or a deacon should be *the husband of one wife*, would seem effectually to quash any contention that the apostolic and post-apostolic priesthood was forbidden to marry. On the other hand, Paul's equally clear desire, expressed in his first letter to the Corinthians, that other servants of God remain, like Paul himself, unmarried, precludes the inference that in speaking of episcopal qualifications he is setting down an imperative in favor of marriage. As the experts would have it, Paul's advice here is restrictive, but not injunctive. Nevertheless, the main issue, the issue raised by Peter's mother-in-law and by the four daughters of Philip, foremost, after Stephen, of the seven first deacons, would appear to be settled by Paul's casual phrase. The first Christian priests could and often did marry.

What does not follow from this handsome admission is that in the first three centuries virginity was not held in high honor or that a considerable number of clerics did not voluntarily embrace chastity. Any interested reader may find in the Catholic Encyclopedia the convincing testimonies of such early writers as Tertullian, Eusebius, Origen, St. Epiphanius and a historian named Socrates to the effect that a strong feeling already existed in favor of voluntary clerical celibacy.

The first recorded ecclesiastical legislation on the subject of celibacy occurs at the very end of the third century, and thus began that stubborn and protracted battle within the stronghold of the Church itself which abundantly indicates the exceedingly vital and critical nature of the whole issue. For eight long centuries the battle raged: quite asexual passions flamed, wounds were dealt and suffered, laws were made and set aside, high commands were issued, obeyed, defied, retracted and issued again, some priests and their fellows lived like typical monks of the desert while some bishops and their sons lived like typical men of the world, the victory leaned first to one side and then the other. Finally, in 1123, the First Lateran Council, meeting at Rome under Pope Callistus II, officially and formally declared the marriages of clerics to be invalid. No one could be so foolish as to suppose that from that moment the entire problem of clerical celibacy was sweetly and completely solved; but from that moment the Roman clergy became *de jure* fully celibate, as the Roman Catholic clergy has remained ever since.

The discussion thus far places one truth beyond the range of doubt: clerical celibacy is imposed by ecclesiastical law, and not by divine law. Christ our Lord very carefully distinguished between the command not to commit adultery and the suggestion to embrace chastity. St. Paul, who is generally about as tentative as a tornado, is astonishingly tentative on the subject of virginity; nowhere else, except in First Corinthians where he is discussing this matter, does Paul sound a little like Hamlet trying to make up his mind. (Incidentally, it is precisely because lifelong chastity is a counsel and not a command that no one—repeat, no one—is obliged under pain of serious sin and sure damnation to accept that divine invitation which we call a religious vocation.) Since, then, the law of celibacy was made by Holy Mother Church, the law of celibacy can be unmade by her. The prospect is unlikely.

Unquestionably, clerical celibacy, in common with riding in aircraft, learning the alphabet, singing grand opera, attacking obesity, getting married and writing books, involves certain grave difficulties. Let us calmly and candidly consider them.

The difficulties occasioned by clerical celibacy may be reduced to two. The first trouble is that men bound by chastity will not really be chaste. The second trouble is that they will.

To put the matter simply and bluntly, the history of the Catholic Church is full of depressing records of undeniable failure in clerical chastity. Popes in ages past have had mistresses, some medieval bishops showed more interest in the advancement of their own sons than in the advancement of the Church, parish priests have at times cohabited with their housekeepers, and even today we occasionally hear of a priest throwing up everything and going off to live somewhere as a married man. Moreover, it is not unreasonable to argue that if there be a number of such clerical collapses that we know about, must there not surely be many more which never in any sense see the light of day?

It is quite useless to attempt anything like a wholesale denial of these unlovely and unhappy allegations. In all truth, we who do deeply love the Catholic Church would wish away this darker side of her history; but, as the sane old philosophical slogan runs, *Contra factum non valet ulla argumentatio: No amount of arguing can alter a fact.* Nevertheless, if it is useless to deny the failures in clerical celibacy, it is equally foolish to become unduly alarmed over them. Let us add a few other undeniable facts to the melancholy facts already adduced.

It must never be forgotten in the whole matter of clerical celibacy that the very existence of the obligation itself was for twelve Christian centuries a subject of debate. Every sane man surely realizes that human beings so hate restrictive legislation of any sort that they submit to it with very bad grace (in the periods when they are not in open rebellion) even when the moral obligation stands beyond any shadow of doubt: witness the clear moral precept which forbids adultery. Now when the restriction concerns one of man's most basic, tenacious and most violent appetites, and when, in addition, the restriction is befogged by widespread official and especially unofficial doubt, will any fair-minded person pretend to be surprised if, in practice, the somewhat doubtful restriction is

frequently set aside in favor of the delectable certainty?
The darkest age for clerical celibacy may not have completely ended with the Council of Trent in the sixteenth
century, but the darkness unquestionably then began to
roll back before the advancing light of strict clerical chastity, and the blessed process has never since been reversed.

What of the notorious clerical scandals that do still
periodically occur to shame good Catholics and rejoice, in
base fashion, the embittered hearts of the Church's enemies? Apart from admitting sadly that such tragedies do
happen and, much more sadly, that they always will happen as long as human nature remains damaged, fallible
and essentially unreliable, there would seem to be only one
sensible remark to make in this regrettable connection.
There are in the United States at this moment 45,222
priests. Naturally, in a matter as delicate as this, mathemat-
ical percentages are not available, yet this is precisely the
sort of human contingency in which the universal *impression* of the people of an entire huge country amounts to the
accurate perception of a truth. Does anyone, even the most
hostile bigot, suggest for a moment that the American people are at this moment laboring under the general and
generally strong impression that Catholic priests as a class
are not chaste? It requires no boldness whatever to affirm
categorically that the exact opposite is the case. The whole
reason why the occasional defection of a Catholic priest
from his vow of chastity becomes at once a *cause célèbre*
and a *chronique scandaleuse* and a mortal, burning scandal
to every decent Catholic, Protestant, Jew and pagan in the
country is precisely because such a thing runs directly
counter to what everyone but the haters and the baiters

knows perfectly well about the Catholic priesthood. Such a solid impression is not made on an entire people by their knowledge that Catholic priests are obliged to be chaste. It is made by the sure knowledge of people in cities and towns and villages that the local parish priest whom they see every day *is* chaste.

But what of the interesting possibility that priests are not really as chaste as appearances would suggest? Two answers may be made to this unpleasant suggestion. First, we deal here with a matter so sensitive and so delicate that appearances cannot for long belie the truth. The priest, like Hamlet, is really too much i' the sun. It may be taken as a fact that neither a protracted intrigue nor repeated questionable connections nor even a particularly warm feminine friendship can pass without instant notice and comment in the life of a Catholic priest, for he, as no other man can be, is in every sense the apple of his people's eye. Sometimes, indeed, an innocent but imprudent priest learns with surprise and shock and pain that his chastity must be a mirror, unclouded by the slightest breath, in which his weak and laboring and admiring people may see themselves a little as God sees them. Secondly, why should it be specially doubted that priests, with all the natural and supernatural helps which they particularly enjoy in this slippery matter, are actually doing what many respected single men and women in lay life are clearly and admittedly doing, that is, leading lives of authentic chastity? We earnestly suggest that if Catholics are worried or anti-Catholics suspicious about the chastity of the clergy, both groups are wasting valuable time and valuable energy. The odor which may be detected about any attack on actual clerical celibacy is, in fact, the familiar odor of red herring.

There remains, then, only the second great difficulty with regard to clerical celibacy. If it be denied that priests are not chaste, then it cannot be denied that they suffer all the well-known disastrous effects of lifelong sexual abstinence.

Let us discuss these well-known and so distressing phenomena.

To begin with, everyone knows that men and women who live lives of total chastity are subject to constant and violent sensual temptations of the most revolting sort. To which we reply with unfailing courtesy: Rot. Everyone knows no such thing. We celibates sometimes gather the impression that non-celibates regard the life of chastity as a deal more titillating and parlous than it actually is. No one seems to pause and try to *think* about continence as rationally and unemotionally as one would think about onions or toothpicks or the price of soap. People do not seem to perceive that (for one thing) chastity is as much a *habit* as unchastity. The longer a habit, even a negative or repressive habit, is cultivated, the easier becomes the act or non-act which is involved. Besides, it must be painfully obvious to any grown person with an ounce of sense that many of the most inevitable annoyances and deprivations in this vale of tears trouble us only as long as we sit and think about them. The best advice I, personally, ever received on the subject of chastity came from an old German priest who is now even merrier in heaven than he was on earth (he was a great lover of good beer), and who simply said, "Forget it." Many will doubt that such a thing can be done. Well, it can.

All gross temptation aside, however, must we not grant that lifelong chastity often gradually produces undesirable psychological consequences in the normal man or woman who undertakes such an abnormal mode of existence? Do not such people tend to be frustrated, narrow, crabbed, irritable and given to fits of depression?

Gentle reader, let me speak personally. Every time I hear levelled against chastity this dear old frustration-argument (for it has aged terribly in its short span of life), I think at once, not of priests at all, but of the nuns I have known. I have known young nuns who were very lovely and old nuns who were very lovable. Once, on a bright October day, when a gentleman happened to be sitting in his car outside a convent listening to the broadcast of a World Series game, a sweet young Sister came swiftly out to ask him, please, to lower the volume, because the uproar could be heard in the chapel, where the Sisters were trying to pray. She flashed such a dazzling smile that the gentleman first snatched off his hat, and then turned off the radio entirely. Sister thanked him; but as she turned to go, she asked anxiously, *Is Brooklyn ahead?* And I have stood watching the belching flames of the steel mills of Pittsburgh while an elderly nun remarked with satisfaction, *It's like hell with the lid off, isn't it?* These and many other Sisters I have known, and I would like to shout until the heavens crack that if any women in the world are frustrated, narrow, crabbed, irritable and given to fits of depression, they certainly aren't Catholic nuns. Offhand, I'd say that the really queer ones were mostly either married women or unwilling non-religious virgins. Nowhere on the face of the earth will you hear sweeter or more genuine laughter than in a convent, although I hasten to add that I have many a time and oft heard the heartiest and most purifying kind of guffawing in my own religious family. If we celibates are frustrated, we certainly seem to make the best of a miserable situation. Speaking as one wretched and hopelessly frustrated priest, I should like to announce to anyone who cares to listen that I feel pretty good. In fact, I like my life just fine. If this be frustration I can only murmur, *The same to you, dear reader, and many of them!*

No doubt a discussion of this sort is not really complete without an eloquent passage on the positive advantages of clerical celibacy as opposed to the real or fancied disadvantages. Yet one wonders if such an apologia be needed. St. Paul has recorded once and for all the indisputable certainty that the celibate servant of God can serve his Master more completely and more perfectly simply because he has no wife to serve at all. Equally certain and perhaps more moving is the golden fact of the spontaneous, trustful and almost possessive love which Catholic people, men, women and children, give to their priest. *Hiya, Father* is what the smiling lips say in the streets, in the buses, in the stores; but the smiling eyes are saying, *You are all ours because you don't belong to any one.* It is true that I will never have a son; but I like to walk past the schoolyard and listen to all the little people who run to call me *Father.*

"I came into thy house, and thou gavest Me no water for My feet . . . no kiss of greeting."

LUKE 7:44-45

VIII

SIMON THE PHARISEE

When Simon the Pharisee went to bed that night, he could not have known that he was an immortal boor. He must have known he was a boor, though; our Lord had told him.

We owe a great deal to that beloved physician, St. Luke. If Luke had given us only the high excitement and thunderous rhetoric of the Acts of the Apostles, we would stand hopelessly in his debt; but, besides all that, the good doctor has handed down to us some of the most memorable of our divine Savior's deeds and words and experiences. Without Luke (and, of course, the Holy Spirit) we would not know that Gethsemani saw a sweat of blood, that Herod the younger made a clown of God's Son, that our Lord raised to life a widow's son; without Luke we would also be without some of our best loved Gospel names: the Good Samaritan, the Prodigal Son, the Good Thief.

One colorful and dramatic incident which Luke records in his usual fast-moving style is to be found in his seventh chapter. It is an event which has provided Christians with one of their most vivid pictures of Christ and exegetes with one of their most fascinating puzzles. The story concerns a lady; a lady of easy virtue.

It all began as so many notable events in our Savior's

life began, with an invitation to dinner. Within the strict range of their own kind, the ancient Jews were a distinctly social and sociable people. Hospitality ranked high as a Hebrew virtue, and the dinner-party was such an esteemed and popular institution that the rabbis even approved such entertainment on the Sabbath day. One wonders at once just who did all the very considerable work in connection with such affairs, and the answer is suggested by not a few Gospel passages. The work was done by the women, who would never have dreamed of sitting down to table with their lords and their lords' male guests. Apparently no one much cared whether the women worked on Saturday or not, so long as the men did nothing. It was a wonderful age for half the human race.

The ancient Jewish dinner-party was governed by the strictest sort of protocol. First, there was an elaborate ritual for the reception of guests, a ritual which was not only mannerly and truly courteous, but which was dictated by the conditions of life in a hot, dusty, semi-tropical world. The arriving guest was received at the door by the host himself, and, as we know from other Scripture passages, was greeted with the formal embrace and the kiss of peace. The guest was then ushered into a side-chamber which served as a combined sitting room, waiting room and bathroom. Here the new arrival seated himself and received two specific attentions: his feet were washed by a slave, and his head anointed with a dressing which we would regard rather as a perfume than as an oil. In the case of particularly distinguished persons, these menial but delicate tasks would be performed by the host himself. Thus refreshed, the guest chatted with his fellows until all had arrived and dinner was announced. It is questionable whether or not we are more civilized people now that these gracious customs have yielded to the modern protocol of the dry martini.

The next ceremonial point of the ancient dinner was the order of seating at table. The point was a sore one, as we see from the prominent notice it receives at several places in the Gospel narrative. The Jews of our Lord's day had adopted the Greco-Roman fashion of *reclining* at meals. Low tables were arranged along three sides of a square, and couches were placed along the outside of the square. The guest reclined on his left arm, his head toward the table and his feet extending away from it; the food was managed with the right hand, the ordinary utensils being the fingers. Such a style in dining, though it may not recommend itself to contemporary tastes, instantly clarifies certain accurate observations of the Evangelists: how, at the Last Supper, for instance, St. John, who was reclining on our Savior's right, naturally whispered to Christ by leaning backward against Him; and how, in the present incident, the uninvited lady who sought out our Lord *took her place behind Him at His feet,* as St. Luke notes. The coveted choice places at table seem to have been those at the head of the separate couches, since each couch accommodated three or even five persons, and the seat of honor would be the place at the head of the central couch.

We have no way of knowing where Christ our Lord sat or reclined at this particular dinner-party given by Simon the Pharisee, but every other circumstance would suggest that He was relegated to the lowest and most undesirable location. If it be so, our Savior made no comment. He took the place assigned Him, addressed Himself to the animal business of eating like the true man that He was, and joined in the formal and somewhat heavy dinner conversation which was the style at Jewish feasts. Apparently, on this occasion no one paid any particular attention at all to our Savior until the sensational interruption occurred.

A woman appeared in the arched entrance to the dining-room and stood for a moment looking sharply about her. She was young; she was no doubt handsome, perhaps strikingly so. No one paid much attention. For one thing, it was a curious item of Hebrew festivity customs that the dining room stood open to casual passersby who might want to admire the occasion and envy the guests. For another, anyone who noticed the girl poised lightly there in the archway might have supposed her a servant or a slave. As she moved swiftly across the floor to the place where Christ our Lord reclined, a few questioning glances were no doubt thrown her way. Only, however, when she silently slipped to the floor at the feet of the prophet from Galilee and He sat erect, facing her, did the murmur of dinner conversation fade out as every eye riveted on the kneeling girl. A sharp buzz of masculine talk suddenly sprang up again and as suddenly died away, now into a taut, expectant silence, for the quick, glittering eyes had not only marked the newcomer, but they had recognized her. The festive dinner had become festive indeed as the pious diners licked their lips in delicious anticipation of being thoroughly shocked and scandalized. The prophet, it seemed, had acquired some very peculiar friends.

There ensued a wordless scene which has branded itself with tenderness upon the Christian memory. The prostrate girl's head rested upon the feet of Christ, her arms were about His legs, her shining, dark hair flowed over all, concealing her face. Her shaking shoulders made it clear that she was crying, but no sound came from her. After a little the dark head was raised, so that anyone could see the gleaming streaks of tears on the feet of the prophet. The woman's hands went to her hair; with it, as with a towel, she dried the feet that she had washed with her tears. Now she knelt erect. The clear, thin tinkle of breaking crystal sounded in that utter silence, and the fine fragrance of expensive perfume floated through the room. Gradually the dark head sank down again. The girl ended her sublime ceremony as she had begun, with her head pillowed on the feet of Christ.

The men sitting at table looked at one another. Still no one spoke. Then a very quiet voice said, almost casually, *Simon, I have a word for thy hearing.*

Simon the Pharisee cleared his throat. He answered carefully, *Master, tell it me.*

There was a creditor who had two debtors, one owed him five hundred pieces of silver, the other fifty; they had no means of paying him, and he gave them both their discharge. Christ, God's Son, sat for a moment quietly regarding the girl at His feet. Suddenly His eyes swung round to His host, and His voice was a shade less silky. *And now tell Me, which of them loves him the more?*

The conundrum was too easy. Whatever else this fellow from Galilee was or was not, He was no fool. Simon the Pharisee spoke warily: *I suppose that it is the one who had the greater debt discharged.*

Thou hast judged rightly. Our Savior turned again to

the prostrate girl. The quiet, easy voice resumed, but the words fell about Simon the Pharisee like so many whips as Christ the courteous guest published for all the ages the calculated boorishness of Simon the host, as Christ the judge compared unfavorably a proud Pharisee with a weeping *fille de joie. Dost thou see this woman? I came into thy house, and thou gavest Me no water for My feet; she has washed My feet with her tears, and wiped them with her hair. Thou gavest Me no kiss of greeting; she has never ceased to kiss My feet since I entered; thou didst not pour oil on My head; she has anointed My feet, and with ointment.* Then Christ our Lord gave to all of us that strange and mysterious principle which, despite all its mystery, has been for so long the dear comfort of so many: *I tell thee, if great sins have been forgiven her, she has also greatly loved. He loves little, who has little forgiven him.*

We are not now concerned with the great love of our Savior's celebrated penitent, nor with the much that had been forgiven her. We are interested in the small love of Simon the Pharisee, and especially in the small and miserable crime which may or may not have been forgiven him. We would like to talk about the small sin of bad manners.

Perhaps we ought to begin by openly skirting a certain pitfall in this matter into which our Victorian ancestors are widely alleged to have fallen: we will not equate manners and morality, we do not suggest that polished exterior behavior implies a shining interior state of soul or unsullied purity of heart. Hamlet's stepfather was courtly in his manners, and Lady Macbeth proved such a charming hostess that King Duncan made certain to send her a diamond ring, by way of heartfelt thanks, just before the Lady and her husband took care of him for once and for all. It might even be urged that there is no strict or strictly direct connection at all between manners and religion; we may be sure that many a crude Christian, as well as many a howling savage, will blunder his honest way into the kingdom of heaven. Manners are the external counterpart and visible indication of what we call civilization. Pigs lined up at a trough have a certain mode of eating, happy cannibals reaching into the pot for the missionary's forearm have a different style, men and women dining on the Starlight Roof of the Waldorf-Astoria have yet another. The primary question raised by the eating habits of these varied feeders is not what religion they practice, since the cannibal, at least, might be far more devout in his odd way than some few of the diners in the Waldorf. The question here is simply whether or not these eaters are human, and, if so, how human.

There remains, of course, a clear and definite, though indirect, connection between religion and manners, a connection which is highly suggestive. It is sometimes suspected and even hinted that the end and object of polished manners is to make an impression on other people. Nothing could be farther from the truth. The end and object of any sane code of manners is to show consideration for other people. A connection exists, therefore—and what a pity it is that Christians do not more generally see this—between manners and the fundamental Christian precept of love of one's neighbor. Bad manners are rarely a mortal sin, but bad manners are invariably a venial violation of fraternal charity.

One of the truly striking characteristics of contemporary Christian civilization is the undeniable decline of manners. Our age rebelled, not indeed without reason, against the strict and elaborate protocol of Victorian manners as against a code which glorified appearance above actuality and which therefore could only be, at bottom, a petrification of sham and artificiality. Honest people did honestly object to the obligation of referring to a female leg as a limb, seeing that trees also possess limbs which assuredly are not legs. People likewise could not rid themselves of a sense of foolishness in rigidly describing pregnancy as a delicate condition, since pregnant cats and dogs (not to mention countless splendid women) gave not the slightest indication of any special delicacy, distress or pathology, but only appeared to be quite thoroughly enjoying their expanded and expanding situation. So the enlightened and emancipated men and women of the twentieth century— an era, be it ever remembered, which was to be truly scientific and no longer merely *arty*—moved to free themselves from the tyranny and falsity of nineteenth century manners. In a familiar and outmoded but yet entirely accurate figure of speech, we threw the baby out with the bath. We made certain to have no artificial manners by having no manners at all.

The kindly and Christian and mannerly reader will naturally bridle at the exaggeration contained in such a a sweeping generalization. Indeed, there *are* gracious manners to be observed in the world about us; in order to witness them you only have to be most assiduously and perseveringly observant, and you must either travel a great deal or not at all. Those who would deny that proper manners have all but vanished from our daily world are invited to recall a casual half-dozen rules of civilized behavior which were universally accepted and almost universally practiced (except, of course, by those who *wanted* to advertise themselves as barbarians) two short generations, that is, fifty short years ago. Men never sat while women stood; men never used even profane language in the presence of women; women always spoke, in public, in a low and "refined" voice; boys addressed older men as *sir*; young girls never uttered certain crude if Chaucerian monosyllables; small children were quiet when with their elders. Has anyone any further remark to make on the subject of the decline of manners?

No doubt there are people who feel simply relieved to be quit of such modes of behavior as we have but now enumerated. Very well, then. This reporter can only remark with considerable sadness that the mere, slight listing of these gracious customs of the past causes him, who is yet far from venerable, a sharp nostalgia for an age of the world which may have been stiff and stuffy, but certainly was not savage. For our current fashion of destroying the niceties of human existence or at least of human behavior is indeed savage in the strictest sense. Like savages, we destroy what we do not understand; like savages we destroy without knowing why; like savages we destroy without ever building again.

It will be observed, in the easy catalogue of civilized habits which were listed above, that manners frequently, though by no means always, bear some special reference to women and children. The point is a provocative one. Commending himself earnestly to his Creator, this person states it as a flat, unqualified and completely undeniable fact that the true culprits, in the whole criminal destruction of courteous manners, are the women of our time.

A fundamental truth of human nature is that men do not instinctively like legislated modes of behavior at all. A man's deepest natural desire is to act as he lists, without reference to any law or principle which would hinder him from doing what he likes at the moment and in the manner of his choosing. Divine commands and the obvious serious inconveniences attached to uncontrolled behavior have moderately persuaded men to accept a code of morality. Take it as a fact, however, that this is as far as the great mass of men are willing to go in the matter of legislated behavior. The average man will commonly keep his hands off another man's wife; but unless he is somehow made to do so, he will not commonly keep his coat on just because she is in the same room.

With women the case is quite otherwise. Women always care for modes or degrees where men only care for the essential fact. In other words, where men will be ruled by morality, women will be ruled by morality and by taste. It might be added that women are sometimes ruled by taste when they are not ruled by morality.

As a consequence, women, if they have not always been the legislators of manners, have always been the observant and vigilant and determined arbiters of manners in the sense that they have been the ones to enforce the code that has once been admitted. If children have no manners today, it can only be because women have not taught them to have manners. If men have no manners today, it is because women have acquiesced in the perennial male hankering for comfortable and selfish barbarism. If women have no manners today, it is because women are less womanly than they were.

Precisely here we ought all to pay open and grateful tribute to one noble army of women who continue valiantly to do battle with the creeping barbarism of our day. The nuns of our nation—those great-hearted women of all ages and colors and types, in their familiar habits of black and brown and blue and white, whom the Catholic faithful, by a sure instinct, call always *the good Sisters*—deserve well of both Church and country under many solid titles of merit. We may all be astonished to discover, in the clear light of revelation that will follow the last trump, that nuns, who are supposed to know little or nothing about the sort of navigation in question, were mainly responsible for keeping our ship of state, leaky and battered and mutinous as it is, from foundering completely on the shoals of national and international crises. However doubtful to many such a reasonable theory may seem to be, it is certain beyond all question that the busy nuns throughout our country are just about the last and only ones who, with heroic and indomitable persistence, are still trying to keep children and young people polite and mannerly. I dare say that one of the sure signs by which you may know that this young woman has attended Miss Vandercliff's and Miss Multibucks' exclusive Avon Dell Country School for Girls is the young lady's gracious manners. This feat is successfully engineered by the Misses Vandercliff and Multibucks in four short years at the cost of only two thousand dollars a year. Mr. and Mrs. Gilhooley, however, will send their young Mary Eileen to the parochial school and then to the nearby Academy of St. Joseph, where the Sisters will turn out a Mary Eileen with perfectly lovely manners at the rate of a couple of hundred dollars a year. No doubt about it, even without birth-control Catholic parents are able to save a bit, here and there, and lose nothing at all by the saving.

May the happy writer (he is always happy when he thinks about Sisters) here indulge in a public and priestly confession? The priest, as he walks the streets, is comforted and cheered to receive many little marks of love from the Catholic faithful. As for one priest, nothing so nearly makes his heart jump with warm joy as a sidewalk curtsey from a little girl. I love it. I love the little girl who does it so quickly and easily. I love the Sisters who taught her to do it; who alone, you may be sure, taught her to do that sweet and grave and yet girlish thing. In other schools the kids learn to rhumba.

No one can possibly guess what the manners of the future among civilized men will be. One could wish that in this matter human behavior will follow the pattern of a cycle, in which event the twenty-first century will be positively courtly in its manners. The writer grieves that he cannot stir up more genuine personal enthusiasm for such a prospect. For one thing, his interest, by and large, in the twenty-first century, with all its pomps and works, tends to be moderate and even cool. Secondly, he sadly regards the cycle-theory of manners as so much eyewash. The problem and challenge for all of us lies not in the next century, when our dust will unquestionably be most re-

fined, but here and now: on our doorstep, in the streets
and in our homes and in our offices. The unavoidable fact
is that good manners can and should be an exercise of
Christian charity. It is a mortal pity, of course, that the
English word which derives from the Latin *caritas* has lost
so much of its tang and vigor in the crush of multiple and
well organized charitable agencies, but the term will never
cease to mean *love*, and love must surely include consideration for our neighbor: not for that theoretical and universal neighbor who exists only in books and precepts, but
for that terribly real and particular neighbor who sits next
to us, talks to us, and generally gets on our nerves. There
are a number of obvious ways in which, for practical pur-
poses, we cannot *love* that fellow, our flesh-and-blood
neighbor. We can, however, be mannerly toward him. We
actually can love him that much, anyhow.

Christ our Savior complained of the bad manners of
Simon the Pharisee, noting in detail Simon's careless crudi-
ties, and making it perfectly clear that He, the Word
Incarnate and the King of glory, felt distinctly hurt by
such boorishness. We might reflect, upon occasion, that
the hurt and accusing eyes of that same Christ are fixed
upon us, and a similar detailed rebuke is springing to His
lips. We will, naturally, return our Lord's reproachful look
with a pose of most elaborate and affecting surprise. Christ
Jesus will not be put off, however. He will say quietly but
very firmly: *As long as you did it to the least of these, you
did it to Me.*

And thereupon all the townspeople went out to meet Jesus; and when they found Him, they entreated Him to leave their country.

MATTHEW 8:34

IX

THE MEN OF GERASA

It certainly gives one an odd and uncomfortable feeling to read that Christ our Lord was once ordered out of a place. Queer . . .

＊

According to a very ancient usage among Christian men and writers, the individual incidents in the life of our divine Savior, God's Son, are spoken of as *mysteries*. The terminology is apt to be perplexing, chiefly because of the change that has occurred in the ordinary meaning of the word *mystery*. A mystery nowadays is either a literary thing (Who murdered the millionaire sportsman, Reginald Rosterwell, and stuffed his dismembered body into the deep-freeze?) or a scientific thing (What causes the common cold?). In both cases the mystery is an event or a fact which we do not understand *as yet*. In the old religious sense, however, a mystery was an event or a fact which men did not understand and never would understand because its full significance lay beyond human comprehension. The happenings of our Lord's life were therefore mysteries, because God-made-man was Himself an impenetrable mystery, and the mystery naturally overflowed into everything He did.

Among the mysteries or events of our Savior's life, some

are most consoling, some are extremely challenging, some are surprising, and some few are puzzling to the point of bewilderment. We cannot afford to forget, as we read the four Gospels, that Christ always acted like God: He acted without consultation or apology, and, at times, with a certain breath-taking indifference as to whether or not His action would be fully understood. The Son of God came on a high mission, and He fulfilled His mission strictly according to the inviolable plan eternally and infallibly drawn up in the timelessness of the Triune Divinity. Our Lord came to tell us something, not to ask our advice. He came to do something, and no creature but one was in any sense consulted on the mode of doing it.

There is possibly no more mysterious mystery in the entire range of the four Gospels than that which took place on the less frequented eastern shore of the Sea of Galilee near a town or in a district which is given a slightly different name by each of the three Synoptics, Matthew, Mark and Luke. Even today the site of this odd wonder lies unknown. St. Matthew says the event occurred in the land of the Gadarenes, but we know today that it could not have happened near the town called Gadara. Mark places the affair in the district of the Gerasenes, but we now know it could not have happened at the town of Gerasa. Luke calls the spot the country of the Gergesenes, and no such locality is at present known at all. Complaint has been made that the Evangelists were not very good reporters in the modern journalistic sense. How true that is! The four biographers of our Lord were so calmly and simply and reasonably engrossed with the terribly significant events that had happened that they frequently did not particuìarly notice where or when they were happening. Can you imagine the expression on St. John's face if anyone had asked him how old Judas was at the time of the betrayal?

What is certain is that the miracle of Gerasa—for convenience, let us call it that—took place on the eastern shore of the Lake of Genesareth at a spot where some sort of precipice falls directly away to the sea; and that it occurred in the period of time well after the Galilean idyll, when our Savior's ministry in Galilee was mounting to its climax and turning-point. The prodigy consisted essentially in the expulsion of an entire gang of evil spirits from a man's body and soul, but the real mystery resides in the odd sequel to the essential point.

In the face of ever-increasing and increasingly bitter opposition, our Savior in His Galilean ministry had just completed a distinct period of preaching which was marked by the suddenly abundant use of the literary device called the parable. Possibly because of the useless annoyance of growing opposition and certainly because of the exhausting pressure of endless work, our Savior with His disciples quietly embarked in their fishing-skiffs and made a night crossing from the west to the east shore of the Lake. The voyage was eventful, for during that night there occurred the celebrated calming of the storm at sea.

Upon disembarking the following morning the little party was met by an individual who would hardly have qualified as a welcoming committee. The man was totally naked; he was apparently huge; he was unquestionably fierce. The poor fellow lived half-way between death and life in the unimaginable filth and degradation of the limestone caves which served the district as a graveyard. St.

Mark's description is clear: the man was a masochistic yet dangerous maniac who had successfully defied all efforts to restrain him and who now terrorized this lonely countryside. Evidently our Lord and His friends had blundered (sic) into a really dangerous preserve, and we may forgive the disciples a degree of genuine alarm as the madman, with wild shouts and fierce gesticulation, bore down on the newcomers. Our Savior, however, stood calm and unmoved, and the charging wild man's next behavior showed plainly the true nature of his madness. He hurled himself not upon Christ, but at our Lord's feet; his tormented screaming proved no threat, but a frantic plea. To the complete amazement of the disciples the maniac seemed perfectly familiar not only with our Savior's name, but with His real identity. Rocking back and forth on his torn knees and clawing at his own breast, the pitiful human wreck kept screeching, *Why dost Thou meddle with me, Jesus, Son of the most high God? I adjure Thee in God's name, do not torment me!*

It was an exciting moment. The followers of our Lord must have gaped, indeed. They had been afraid of the madman, but the madman was far more afraid of their Master. Suddenly they understood: the fellow was a victim of diabolical possession; with his voice the unseen demons were shrieking their capitulation as the true strong Man of the parable, armed with unutterable holiness, came upon them to their destruction. As always in His direct dealings with evil spirits, our Savior is brief, imperious, contemptuous. To all the demented screaming He has but one brief reply: *Go out of him.* Then follows the odd thing, and let Matthew tell it in his own words: *Some distance*

*away, a great herd of swine was feeding; and the devils
asked a favor of Him; If Thou hast a mind to cast us out,
they said, send us into the herd of swine. He said to them,
Away with you; and they came out and went into the herd
of swine; and with that, all the herd rushed down the cliff
into the sea, and perished in its waters.*

We may well wonder whether, in the whole wide range
of the Gospel story, there is another event as vivid and as
astounding as this. The bizarre incident has, of course,
differently affected different readers. Those who love our
Lord are respectful but baffled. Those who hate Christ
have quickly recovered from their own astonishment to
leap with shouts of glee upon this narrative and claw it
to pieces. The adverse critics have fallen roughly into two
classes: those who say the Gospel account is shocking
because such a thing could not possibly have happened
and those who say the Gospel account is shocking because
such a thing did most certainly happen. Let us leave these
excited critics happily contradicting one another, for they
truly represent no concern of ours at the moment. Catholic
scholars have patiently pointed out, a) that the raising of
swine was a forbidden occupation in any part of Palestine,
b) that any number of dumb animals, even granting that
some of them are far more appealing and sensible than
their noisiest human friends, may rightly be sacrificed to
the authentic good of one human being, c) that our Savior
may have reimbursed the owners of the swine in ways
which are not told us, and d) that in the final analysis the
supreme Lord of all creation enjoys the unchallengeable
right to dispose of His creatures in any way He wishes, for

His own good ends, and in anyone's immediate despite.

Nothing of all this touches upon our present interest; for our purpose we must return to the Gospel narrative. The stupified swineherds, as soon as their popping eyes sank back into their heads, simply bolted. They rushed into the nearby town (whatever its name was) and retailed their story to the incredulous citizenry. Naturally, no one believed them, and, quite understandably, the entire town turned out and went back with the swineherds to the rocky lakeside. They did not see any pigs, but they saw something much better, indeed something which represented a very considerable benefaction to the whole neighborhood. Their local nudist madman, who had so effectually terrorized the district, was sitting quietly and fully clothed at the feet of a stranger whose name was Jesus and who hailed from Galilee across the lake. Obviously there followed interrogations (querulous but cautious) and explanations (serene and quite cheerful), conferences and caucuses, negotiations and proposals, of all of which we hear nothing. Finally the local gentry made up their minds. *They entreated Him to leave their country* (Matthew). *Whereupon they began entreating Him to leave their country* (Mark). *Then all the common folk of the country round Gerasa asked Jesus to leave them* (Luke). It is sufficiently clear that the writers, as well as the readers, of the Gospels are shocked by this affair, but it is equally clear that the Evangelists are not wasting tears over swine. Theirs is the real shock in this shocking narrative.

When the men of Gerasa ordered Christ out of their country, they set a sad precedent which Christian men have been following, on and off, more or less, ever since. Let us consider this matter.

Christ God, now sitting in His glorified humanity at the right hand of His Father, no longer needs a country or a piece of geography in which to operate for the salvation of mankind. When the Son of God came among us men in the body of this flesh, He accepted, along with all the other normal circumstances of humanity, the spatial condition of living out His mortal life in a defined and even highly confined sector of the earth's surface. It is astonishing, when one pauses to think of it, how very little of the world our Savior actually saw—a thought which may serve to console frustrated globe-trotters. Moreover, although He passed His years and did His visible work in a certain place, our Lord never evinced the slightest interest in one place over another—He made a casual remark along these lines to the celebrated Samaritan woman—and whenever He spoke of the kingdom which He would found He made it abundantly clear that that kingdom would have no territorial boundaries. Consequently, it is no longer a critical matter, though it is always as painful as ever, when Christ in His Mystical Body is chased out of a geographical country or over a physical border. Legend has it that certain members of the Society of Jesus, as they were firmly escorted to some frontier or other (for we really have been put out of quite a number of places) were heard cheerfully to remark, *We've been thrown out of better countries than this.* We do not attribute any such Jesuitical flippancy to the Mystical Christ, yet nothing is more certain than that, whenever our Lord is banished from any state or territory, He is already on His way back. Christ in His

Church is not easily discouraged, and certain broad hints He steadfastly ignores.

No, the place that the Son of God cherishes and treasures, the land which He leaves only under the most direct compulsion, and then with an authentic wrench of His Sacred Heart, is the beloved country of Mansoul. The kind reader naturally supposes that we now lapse into colorful metaphor. No such thing. Let us expound.

Any discussion of this vital and somewhat mysterious matter must necessarily begin with the familiar catechism question, *Where is God?* We all remember the easy and veritable answer: *God is everywhere*. Moving naturally from the first catechism to the *Summa Theologica* of St. Thomas Aquinas, we learn that God is present everywhere, and therefore in the soul of man, in three ways: by His power, since every created thing without exception is subject to God's immediate and present dominion; by His actual nearness, since all things are instantly open and known to Him; by His essence, since nothing can remain in existence without His sustaining presence. In this triple sense God is actually everywhere: in my hand as I write, in the pencil with which I write, in the desk at which I write. In a yet nobler sense, however, God is or should be present in a man's soul.

The highest gift of God to man is the gift of sanctifying grace. Of sanctifying grace, as of the Divine Majesty itself, it is easier to say *that* it is than to say *what* it is. Sanctifying grace is a purely supernatural reality which almighty God freely and generously infused into the souls of the first man and woman, which they lost for themselves and their posterity by the wilful criminality of original sin, and which is yet again freely and generously infused into the human soul at the moment of Baptism in the name of the Father, the Son and the Holy Spirit. Sanctifying grace is best understood through its astounding and even unbelievable effects. For example, with the advent of sanctifying grace the Triune God comes instantly to take up His actual, personal, intimate and most loving abode in a man's soul. God thus becomes present in a human being in a sense which goes inexpressibly beyond His presence in a rock or a tree or in the unbaptized soul. God is now present in a man not only by His power and His everywhereness and by His being what He is; that is, God is no longer present in a man only by a kind of essential necessity; He is now present by invitation and acceptance, by mutual desire, by love. God's union with the soul is now that of the purest lover.

One further amazing beauty of this amazing truth is that when the Supreme Being enters thus into a man as an eager Friend and Father and Brother, He comes on no fleeting or limited visit. He comes to stay. Indeed, this invisible union of God with man is simply the beginning of that visible, ineffable union which will make man supremely and perfectly and endlessly happy in heaven.

Unfortunately, there arises one difficulty. There is a flaw in this gorgeous actuality, there is a fly in this heavenly ointment. Man would not be man without the true freedom of his will, and therefore it lies constantly in man's decision whether this union with God will continue or not. Since God comes in sanctifying grace as one who is loved and wanted, He will obviously stay only as long as He is loved and wanted. The most terrible power that the rational creature possesses is the dreadful power to say to the God dwelling within him, *Get out!*

How is the appalling power exercised? By an act of the free human will; by that act which Catholic terminology calls mortal sin.

Such terminology is not popular nowadays. It is commonly understood that the sisters who teach in parochial schools spend most of their time screaming at their pupils about mortal sin, and I have glanced at a tenth-rate novel in which the little children of a Catholic family, hagridden by the fear of hell, were always stopped dead in their tracks by the parental bellow that whatever the youngsters were about to do was a mortal sin. This I have read, but I have never witnessed anything quite so efficient. Of course, even the word *sin* no longer figures largely in sophisticated usage, for what used to be called sin is now termed anti-social behavior. If a man, in a fit of pique, knocks his mother-in-law down a flight of stairs, he is not now said to have committed a sin or, indeed, done anything especially wrong. He is guilty of anti-social behavior, although mother-in-law, when and if she regains that power of speech which really and in a most exact sense precipitated the whole affair, may seem inclined to employ harsher terms. More obviously, people no longer speak of *mortal* sin even when they talk of sin, simply because they do not know what the adjective means in that context.

The word mortal derives from the Latin *mors*, which means *death*, and so *mortal* means *lethal*. The act of mortal sin is a lethal act because it destroys the supernatural life of the soul. It is a pity, of course, that the dead soul of man does not visibly and offensively manifest its true condition as man's dead body does, but then the whole world of the supernatural is not gross and palpable as the material and natural world is. A certain subtlety is one of the essential marks of the true supernatural, from which fact we may conclude that roaring evangelism, snake-handling and foaming transports lack something of a genuinely religious quality. Nevertheless, the soul in mortal sin is dead, supernaturally but actually dead. What does such a condition mean? Ultimately, it means that if the man meets death in this unchanged and unrepented state and thus comes to stand before the just tribunal of God for judgment, he must be condemned to the torments of hell forever. Immediately, supernatural death means that through the gaping wound made by mortal sin sanctifying grace has drained out of the soul far more instantaneously and completely than a man's blood drains from a slit throat or a split chest. It means, above all, that the Triune God—the loving Father, the redeeming Son, the indwelling Spirit—has departed. Now is man in far more pitiful case than the cow or the cabbage or the clod of earth. He had been a temple of the most high God, and now the temple lies in ruins, all ravaged and untenanted. Like blinded Gloucester in *King Lear*, the soul in mortal sin is *all dark and comfortless*.

The real misunderstanding about grievous or mortal sin is the failure to grasp that mortal sin is an offense against a *Person*. It is hardly to be expected that the average man will in any sense grieve over the simple fact of the violation of law. Man does not naturally like law, and the flat violation thereof leaves him cold, as the successful and difficult evasion of law puts him in a glow. Sin is too much thought of, when people think about it at all, as an understandable and passing failure to comply with a precept which, under the circumstances, became exceedingly difficult and therefore not quite reasonable. We who believe in God and His Christ must somehow regain and recultivate the simple, clear realization that grievous sin is not just a lapse against a code, but a slap in the face. Mortal sin is a personal insult: a calculated defiance of and a flagrant rebellion against a loving and now sorrowing Father. It is neither extravagant nor sentimental, but only literal truth, to say that serious sin does not merely break a rule; it breaks a heart: the Sacred Heart.

The other misconception about mortal sin is the odd impression which is sometimes found among the most unlikely people, that grave sin must somehow involve some sort of direct, positive hatred of God. The logical conclusion to such thinking must be that there is, in effect, only one mortal sin, the sin of formal blasphemy. It would follow also (and this is what clearly prompts the whole train of thought) that sin which is committed somewhat hesitantly or reluctantly or with a strong concomitant element of regret is not really serious sin. The truth is that such sin is rather especially serious sin, for it implies clear perceptions and very definite prior reflection. Real mortal sin can be committed and frequently is committed with a deal of regret, but what counts is not the vague regret, but the very concrete act which is *de facto* performed. The essence of sin is that sin is a choice: a choice of something which at this moment I want more than I want God. Such a choice may well be made with considerable misgiving, but the question is, Was it made?

Perhaps the most striking part of the sad story of the men of Gerasa is the end of it. They told Christ to get out, and, without a word, He got out. It would be better for a man who commits mortal sin if God were to leave him with a protest or a threat or even with a curse. But as soon as the human will embraces the evil thing, God departs in a silence that is complete, awful, frightening. We might, in our sin, even feel better if, in going, Christ would only say *something*. But no, that is not true. In mortal sin, nothing can make us feel better; nothing.

"She answered Him: Ah, yes, Lord; the dogs eat of the crumbs the children leave, underneath the table."

MARK 7:28

X

THE SYRO-PHOENICIAN WOMAN

Leave it to a woman to have the last word, even in an argument with the blessed Son of God.

That narrow, eastern-Mediterranean strip of land which bears the name of Palestine was once known as the land of Canaan. Scholars tell us that the name *Canaan* probably meant *Land of the purple*; for the ingenious inhabitants of that coastline had discovered that from the secretions of an abundant local shellfish could be made a deep red dye, and the discovery had added a most coveted item to the luxury trade of the ancient world. Scarlet robes—for the ancient *purple*, like that of a modern bishop, was far more red than blue—became standard wear for princes, conquering warriors and distinguished men generally on their most distinguished occasions; hence the savage irony of the fouled old scarlet cloak that was thrown over Christ during the brutal sport of the first Good Friday morning. Among the then up-and-coming Greeks the word for purple or scarlet was *phoinos*, and they began to call their eastern, dye-selling neighbors *Phoenicians*.

The Canaanites or Phoenicians were originally Semitic, and were unquestionably among the most gifted people of the shadowy pre-Western world. From the Phoenicians the alert Greeks learned the alphabet: the Greek word for *book—biblios*—from which we have *Bible*, was simply the name of an influential Canaanite city. From the Phoenicians the Hebrews learned all their music, and when Solomon undertook the building of the Temple he contracted for lumber and woodcutters from a prince of Phoenicia, whom he subsequently diddled nicely on the whole deal. From the Phoenicians, also, the children of Israel occasionally borrowed helmeted, short-skirted deities like Baal to tide them over dull periods when they grew bored with the Lord God of armies, the God of Abraham, Isaac and Jacob.

The time had been when the Canaanites had inhabited the whole corridor of land between Egypt on the south and Syria on the north, but the Israelite invasion had driven them slowly into the north and finally pinned them to a narrow strip of coastline on the northwest; for the Canaanites seem always to have been a westward-looking people, seafarers and traders rather than nomads and sheep-herders in the Oriental fashion. Even in the time of our Lord, although there were roads from Phoenicia to Israelite Galilee, there was relatively little intercourse between the two peoples. The Phoenicians were still pagan, were still contemptuously labeled *Canaanites* by the Jews, were still held in that lordly abomination which the chosen people bestowed so freely on all non-Jews. It must have been with considerable astonishment that our Savior's disciples heard from Him the announcement, soon after the explosive healing of the paralytic at the Bethesda pool in the second year of the public life, that they would make a journey into the region of Tyre and Sidon, the two chief cities of Phoenicia.

Actually, that particular journey of our Lord's was surprising in more ways than one. To begin with, for the first time since, as an infant, He was carried into the exile of Egypt, Jesus goes beyond the boundaries of His native land into really foreign and infidel territory. Secondly, the journey stands unique among all His major peregrinations in being not at all a missionary expedition. He Himself will tell us most explicitly that He had not entered Phoenicia in order to preach or proselytize or do any apostolic work; and St. Mark, who had the story from Peter, who was there, insists on the same point: *There He went into a house, and did not wish anyone to know of it.* The fact is that our Savior was making what the military people call a strategic withdrawal. He has definitely passed the highwater mark of His Galilean popularity, He is practically a proscribed public enemy in all-important Judea, His steps are dogged by spies and informers, Herod the fox has but recently done the Baptist to death and might be in a mood for any wild savagery. Yet the appointed hour of our Savior's sacrifice has not yet struck, and so much of the essential training of the Apostolic College remains to do. Christ our Lord follows the sensible counsel He will give to His followers of all the ages, and quietly slips away from the place and time of serious trouble.

The ruse was moderately successful, for our blessed Lord did succeed in escaping all the powerful men who wanted to kill Him. He did *not* succeed in escaping one quite ordinary woman who merely wanted to consult Him. Perhaps, however, we do an injustice to describe this particular female as ordinary. She may be nameless but she is memorable; beyond doubt, one of the most indelible women of the Gospel story.

Under circumstances of which we know nothing, our Savior and His disciples had found a lodging amid their strange surroundings. Apparently they were not long off the road, and, if so, the weary bustle of settling down was still in process, when suddenly the door opened and a strange woman entered. The newcomer was not only female and strange, but also manifestly non-Jewish; we may imagine that the tired apostolic faces which turned toward her were not exactly beaming with welcome. The lady, with that monomaniac aplomb of which few men are really capable, coolly looked about her, and then unhesitatingly advanced to where Jesus was standing. She began to cry in a loud voice—so says St. Matthew, and we rather get the impression that the good woman had one of those voices which ring, if they do not sing, in the ear: *Have pity on me, Lord, Thou Son of David. My daughter is cruelly troubled by an evil spirit.* The only surprising element in the plea was the very Jewish mode of address; perhaps the woman had heard our Savior described in these terms. The phenomenon of diabolical possession was perfectly well known to the pagans, as anyone may see by reading the *Ajax* of Sophocles. The real surprise in this whole affair comes in the truly unusual behavior of our Lord. He stood for a moment looking at the woman, and then, without a word, turned away from her and continued with whatever He had been doing.

There followed an extraordinary and highly painful scene. Evidently the poor distressed lady trailed around the room after our Lord, wailing and crying; evidently she occasionally addressed or attached herself to various disciples who might have unwarily looked sympathetic for a moment. This is one of those amazing moments in the Gospel narrative when Christ is the only undisturbed person in a scene which is either convulsed or quite mad. Finally the disciples could stand the tension no more. There is no indication that they felt particularly sorry for the pagan woman. St. Matthew does *not* say that they asked Jesus to grant the petition; he merely reports the apostles as pleading, *Get rid of her*—and they do use the imperative. After the exact manner of the timeless and placeless male, they were sick of listening to a strange woman howling; they wanted, after their journey, to eat in peace and afterwards to sleep in peace.

Our Savior, perhaps now seated, answers the disciples with quiet firmness. He was ever insistent that He was, so to speak, under orders, that there was a methodical plan and procedure to the redemption of a world, that certain works must not be done nor certain things said before their proper and appointed hour. His own direct apostolate was limited and defined: the lion's share in the actual physical spreading of His kingdom on earth would be left to other hands than His. Thomas and Matthew and Paul and Boniface and Patrick and Xavier and Isaac Jogues would have their work cut out for them, and our Lord had no intention of doing it for them. He said, making sure, in His utterly priceless way, that the strange lady would hear Him, *My errand is only to the lost sheep that are of the house of Israel.* At that point any mere male petitioner would have departed. The Phoenician lady came forward, fell on her

knees at the feet of Jesus, and said simply, *Lord, help me!*
There was a little pause, and then, speaking very distinctly,
our gentle Savior said a cruel thing; He made the kind of
shattering remark which He makes only to saints and sin-
ners. He said: *Let the children have their fill first; it is not
right to take the children's bread and throw it to the dogs.*
Precisely as the ancient Greeks classed as *barbarians* all
who did not speak Greek, so the people of Israel regarded
all non-Jews as not merely foreigners, but as outcasts.
About such matters the Jews were hearty and explicit:
they commonly called the Gentiles *dogs*, and in the ancient
Oriental world, the dog was by no means man's best friend,
but a mangy pariah cur which possessed no rights because
it enjoyed no respect. The Phoenician woman was not having her knuckles rapped; it was rather more like having
her heart broken.

Christ Jesus, who is great when all others would be
small, who is always practical and never sentimental, who
will never settle for half a loaf when, with the loving turn
of a screw, He stands a chance of getting bakery, baker
and all, knew well the mettle He was testing. The quick-
witted lady is instant with her retort, a retort both bril-
liant and humble: *Ah, yes, Lord; the dogs eat of the
crumbs the children leave, underneath the table.* Joyously
vanquished is the Lion of Judah, and the Hound of Heaven
Himself is happily brought to bay by a dogged Gentile
dog. Our Savior utters a great, contented cry: *O lady!
Great is thy faith; let thy will be granted!—And from that
hour,* concludes St. Matthew with satisfaction, *her daughter was cured.*

The admirable behavior of this pagan woman of the

north might well prove fruitful for many besides her own daughter. It might cure us, too: of a sad misunderstanding in the entire matter of the habitual dealings of God our Lord with us. The misunderstanding is simple, clear and understandable. We think that because God loves us, He wants what is nice for us. He doesn't.

The trouble arises from the intrusion of mere natural sentiment or sentimentality into the more vigorous world of the supernatural: we keep trying to remake our strong Christian God—*Theos ischyros, Deus fortis, strong God*—into the image and likeness of Santa Claus. Sentiment or emotion has been the bane of post-Reformation Christianity as it never afflicted either Judaism, Mohammedanism or early Christianity; compare, for example, the thunder and the gigantic imagery of the Psalms with the wheezing and whining of certain modern hymns which had best go unnamed. Pseudo-Christian pseudo-art, too, has connived at the sentimentalizing process, making a wan, sugary, ineffectual-looking nonentity out of the powerful and almost violent Christ of the Gospels. So we tend to regard the Divine Majesty as a benevolent old gentleman who, if we are good, will certainly bring us whatever we want for Christmas for the reason (to us, excellent) that we want it. It would be much more reasonable and realistic to expect almighty God to take something from us for Christmas for the identical reason: because we want it.

The Santa Claus image of God our Lord is by no means to be corrected by substituting for it a malevolent and tyrannous Zeus or Jupiter. It is as silly to suppose that God primarily desires what is painful to us as to presume that He primarily desires what is pleasant for us. The fact is, as we have all said a thousand times, particularly when someone else is in trouble, that God desires quite simply what is good for us. Obviously, however, the definition of *good* in that familiar formula depends entirely on the end or purpose or objective that is to be achieved in the entire action. And that is precisely where we accidental mortals don't see eye to eye with the Necessary Being. We insist on believing that God is interested in making us happy here and now. He isn't, really. He is really interested in making us happy, so to put it, then and there. This capital point must be clarified. Just what over-all purpose is God our Lord pursuing in His dealings with us, His creatures?

Almighty God has made us for Himself. That is to say: He has brought us into existence, not for any use that we might conceivably be to Infinite Perfection, but quite simply that we might ultimately possess and be possessed by Infinite Perfection through flawless and unending personal union with the God who made us. If it be asked *why* the Creator fashioned us for such an end, the answer is prompt: what other purpose could be worthy of the Infinite Agent and so glorious for us finite recipients? Our final destination is the true interest we hold for almighty God, and, speaking most strictly, it is the *only* interest we hold for Him. Since our ultimate destination depends wholly on our basic supernatural condition in this life, and since the precise degree of our joy or misery in our ultimate destination depends on our present supernatural growth or decay, it follows that God our Lord's sole immediate objective in our regard is to make us grow and prosper on the supernatural level exclusively.

If only we could grasp this vital truth with any degree

of conviction, that the whole sum and complex of perishable facts, events, circumstances and conditions does not really interest God our Father, not because He is a brute, but simply because He knows in His wisdom that this whole sum of things is a sum without finally being a substance, because it is ultimately meaningless! No doubt we will have to be basking merrily in the full blaze of the Beatific Vision before we will be able to realize why that which is now so terribly critical and vital for us should, in itself, have not the slightest final interest for God our most loving Father. However, we might, as a mere therapeutic exercise, try casting our thoughts back five, ten or twenty years so that we might wonder, for an idle and nostalgic moment, what ever did become of those crises which rocked us then like cosmic earthquakes. Ah, gentle male reader, is it not a blessed thing that that pretty, blond and brainless high-school girl did not moon and mope over you as you did over her, these many years ago?

God our Lord, then, in all His deeds and dealings with us, is pursuing a single objective: our supernatural well-being. Everything else without exception, and particularly everything that takes place on the natural or temporal level, concerns and interests our Creator only insofar as it has some bearing on our supernatural robustness. We must struggle to understand that Christ our Lord was no more concerned about the physical health—regarded in itself—of the pagan woman's daughter than He was about the health of some little black girl who at that moment might have been shaking with fever in some hut in equatorial Africa. What Christ did care about, what He did work over, what He did promptly sight and relentlessly pursue was the building up of the supernatural health of the little girl's mother. The pagan woman came to our Lord a spiritually sick woman because she was a pagan, and she left a spiritually well woman because she went away full of supernatural faith. *That* is the story of the Syro-Phoenician woman. The cure of the daughter is a detail, an incident. In this particular drama of the supernatural, that is, of the really real, the little sick-well girl is a stage property.

Perhaps not a few sincere followers of Christ our Lord may be offended by such a harsh commentary on one of our Savior's miracles. We can only respond by pointing to the undeniable harshness of our Lord's deeds and words on this occasion. It is better to experience a certain painful disillusionment on the subject of Christ than to go on harboring any sentimental delusion about Him, His ways and His objectives in our regard. For it must be patent that if I stubbornly insist on misinterpreting God's whole *purpose* in all His dealings with me, I am in for some sad disappointments and not a few jarring experiences in my lifelong relationship with my Maker.

Consider, for example, the whole matter of petitionary prayer. Christ Himself has encouraged and even urged us to practice petitionary prayer and to do so with confidence and perseverance. Possibly it is unfortunate that our habitual prayer tends to be so exclusively impetrative; but certainly it is regrettable that our supplications are so demanding and so absolute. Our Savior unquestionably said, *Ask, and you shall receive.* But that remark, like every other individual statement He made—and how about the exhortation to *hate* mother, father, sister, brother?—is to be received and understood against the broad background and in the full context of everything else He said. So when a tearful lady begs me to offer the Holy Sacrifice of the Mass for the speedy recovery from illness of her mother, aged eighty-six, and to offer the august Sacrifice in honor of the Immaculate Heart of Mary because won't we surely receive anything we ask through Mary's Immaculate Heart?—when this sort of thing happens, I need be nothing more than an ordinary human being in order to feel sorry for the lady, but I need be no more than a mediocre theologian to know with certainty that something is wrong, somewhere, quite apart from mother's rather understandable illness. Where in the world do we Christians pick up the queer notion that almighty God will keep our mothers breathing until they are one hundred and eighty-six simply because we make our request through that poor Blessed Mother who had to watch her own Divine Son die in agony when He was about thirty-three?

In this whole matter there is nothing wrong with God our Father, there is nothing wrong with Christ our Mediator, there is nothing wrong with Mary, help of Christians. There *is* something decidedly wrong with *us*. We do not perceive that we are not full of faith, but touched with superstition, that we show not the slightest interest in any wise plan of almighty God, but are concerned only about our own selfish, wilful desires, that we just want our mothers to stay here on earth with us rather than that we should all happily arrive in heaven with God. It may not be matter for astonishment that we groping mortals are shortsighted, but there is little excuse, even when we are dealing with Our Father who is in heaven, for our being impenetrably stupid and completely unreasonable. Let us indeed supplicate the Divine Majesty for anything and everything we believe to be needful to us. By all means we should pray, pray hard, pray confidently, pray perseveringly; perhaps we will pray tearfully. Just let us try to grasp a simple truth before, while and after we pray, whether with or without tears. If we ask, we will receive; for this we have our Lord's word. But since we will infallibly and inevitably receive only what our wise and loving Father sees will work to our ultimate *supernatural* good, why not ask for just that? At the very least, let us attach this invaluable little recognition as a rider to all our prayers of petition. Like the pagan lady in the land of Phoenicia we will say, *Lord, help me.* But like Christ in the Garden of Olives let us add: *Not my will, but Thine be done.*

The more often you read the strange story of the Syro-Phoenician woman the more you will wonder at the beating she absorbed at the hands of Infinite Love. Of course, it is possible to fasten on the very end of the whole incident and to say, *Well, she did get what she wanted.* She did; but that is not the point. The miracle is not important in this miracle. The heart of this matter is that Christ Jesus by clear implication called a pleading woman a dog. This was not nice of Him. It was only good of Him. Learn this fine distinction from the patient, persevering, pagan lady and you will be in a fair way to know the Incarnate Son of God, not as you might like Him to be, but as He is. In spite of all that we may think in dark moments, Christ our Lord, with His views and His ways, really can't be improved upon.

"They said anxiously to one another, We have brought no bread. Jesus knew it and said, What is this anxiety?"

MARK 8:15-17

XI

THE FORGETFUL DISCIPLES

There is a rather special point which Christ repeatedly insisted on. His disciples did not get the point. Neither, frequently, do we.

A very curious incident took place one day early in the summer of the second year of our blessed Lord's public life. Our Savior had just completed the wide, swinging tour which took Him in a clockwise circle north and west through pagan Phoenicia, east around snow-capped Mount Hermon, and south into the region called Decapolis, on the eastern shore of the Sea of Galilee. He tarried in the Decapolis but briefly; once again He and His people crossed the lovely but unpredictable lake which was so much a part of their lives, and came to rest—gratefully, we may suppose—in their native Galilee.

The welcome which they received was neither what they might reasonably have expected nor what they certainly could have desired. During this absence of our Savior from Israel proper, two powerful groups of His enemies had made shift to bury, temporarily, their own considerable differences in order to make common and therefore more effective cause against Him. The Pharisees, who were puritans, and the Sadducees, who were sceptics, cordially detested one another, but they unhesitatingly set the pattern which would be followed by Pilate and Herod, and, much later, by the various discordant groups who hate the Catholic Church: they briefly suspended their own mutual abhorrence in order to indulge and implement their greater, more urgent hatred. Shortly after our Savior's return, a delegation of Pharisees and Sadducees presented themselves, and, after the manner of sincere seekers for the truth of God, piously asked our Lord for some sign from heaven as a proof of His identity and divine mission.

It really would seem that this was one of the occasions which most sorely tried the patience of our patient Lord. The Pharisaic-Saducean request for a sign was not only puritanic and highly sceptical; in the light of preceding events it was nothing less than brazen effrontery. That period of Christ's ministry which was now mounting to a climax, that happy Galilean idyll, had been marked by a whole series of prodigious miracles. There had been the weird but surely well-reported cure of the demoniac of Gerasa; that calming of a storm at sea of which the disciples must have given to all listeners the most convincing eye-witness account; such public and well-attested events as the raising of the dead daughter of Jairus and the cure of the hemorrhissa; the ceremonious cure of a deaf-mute before a whole crowd of people; and finally, two distinct miraculous repasts of bread and fish which had had a total of considerably more than nine thousand partakers and therefore witnesses. At the end of this series of unheard-of and breath-taking prodigies, the enemies of our Savior ask Him for a sign from heaven. Small wonder that our divine Lord's answer on this occasion was curt, and, as He sounds in Matthew's account, scornful and almost bitter. He brands His questioners as an evil and faithless lot, tells them they can read no signs more subtle than the signs of tomorrow's weather, and flings them but a mysterious scrap of direct answer to their request: they shall have no sign but the sign of Jonas. For them, the next proof which He will offer will be His last: His empty tomb. *And He left them and went away,* Matthew concludes significantly.

St. Mark tells us where our Savior went. Oddly, and as if in disgust, our Lord immediately re-embarked with His disciples, and again crossed the Sea of Galilee, this time heading for the northeastern shore. Somehow one gets the impression from both Gospel accounts that as the skiff nosed its way back across the lake our Savior was silent and withdrawn, and that His mood communicated itself to the disciples; perhaps they spoke to one another in low tones and occasionally shot an inquiring and somewhat apprehensive look at their Lord. Abruptly He said, *See that you have nothing to do with the leaven of the Pharisees and Sadducees.* The figure of speech was neither completely mysterious nor completely unfamiliar. Palestinian yeast was nothing more than old dough whose transforming power made it a ready symbol for corruption, even though our Savior's other recorded use of the figure has a quite opposite meaning. The misunderstanding which followed in the present instance is perfectly descriptive of Christ's major difficulty in dealing with His earnest but earthy followers.

Quite apart from the thunderingly spiritual quality of *what* He had come to reveal, our Lord in His whole *manner* of revelation was, at His most prosaic, a true poet:

symbol and image and figure and metaphor fall naturally and perfectly from His lips. His devoted followers, on the other hand, were nothing if not literal-minded. The subject of whatever whispered colloquies had taken place in that boat that day was an understandable one: the unexpected and unscheduled return across the lake had allowed no time for the purchase of much-needed provisions. We may be sure that the disciples possessed the hearty appetites of grown men who spend most of their time out-of-doors, and there is every indication that they never did become accustomed to our Lord's extremely casual eating habits. Here were twelve already hungry men just starting on a boat trip, and they have only one loaf of bread in the boat. It certainly could be that hard words had already slipped out of the corners of apostolic mouths when Christ suddenly mentioned leaven. The Twelve understood perfectly: they looked at one another with anxious dismay, knowing they were being scolded for forgetting to buy bread. They were not fools; they knew a hawk from a handsaw, and bread from stones.

Well, the disciples had not been rebuked; but they were emphatically rebuked now. As we read St. Mark's account in particular, we marvel even today—and perhaps shiver a little—at the sharpness and profusion of this reprehension of Christ's: *What is this anxiety, that you have brought no bread with you? Have you no sense, no wits, even now? Is your heart still dull? Have you eyes that cannot see, and ears that cannot hear; do you remember nothing? When I broke the five loaves among the five thousand, how many baskets full of broken pieces did you take up? They told Him, Twelve. And when I broke the seven loaves among*

*the four thousand, how many baskets full of broken pieces
did you take up then? And they told Him, Seven. Then He
said to them, How is it that you still do not understand?*

This astounding passage wants careful examination. The
disciples were being lectured, and severely; but the question is, For what? Certainly not for failing to lay in a stock
of food. And does not the reprehension seem a trifle round
for the understandable concern of hungry men who suddenly discover that they are without provision or visible
means of provision?

There would seem to be only two adequate explanations
of this surprising outburst on the part of our gentle Lord.
First, He is disturbed by the prolonged incapacity of His
closest followers, those who have enjoyed the best and the
most of His careful training, for the most rudimentary
spiritual or supernatural thought as distinct from grossly
material concepts and judgments. Much more, Christ is
stung to exasperation by the *anxiety* of His followers. He
blames them, and blames them eloquently, for worrying.
The fact that the worry of the disciples on this occasion
seems quite reasonable to us, together with the consequent
fact that this particular scolding seems therefore excessive,
ought to provide us with the key to this entire incident.
Christ our Lord hates worry with a singular detestation. It
follows that many a modern Christian is not very Christian in the matter of worry.

The first step toward ironing out this prominent and
annoying wrinkle in our Christian lives must be a clear
understanding of what worry really is. For example, people
insist on confusing worry with reasonable concern for

duties and obligations, with the inevitable result that when they are asked not to worry about something, they feel sure that they are being urged not to care a hoot about anything. This confusion of anxiety with conscientiousness is highly instructive for the priest in particular, for it is the elusive root of the neurosis known as scrupulosity. Whatever the explanation of the distinction between worry and conscientiousness, there can be no doubt whatever about the reality of the distinction. Christ our Lord spent a considerable amount of time and truly royal rhetoric urging His followers to attend seriously to their many moral obligations, but He also repeatedly and explicitly condemned anxiety. Actually, the difference between worry and conscientiousness is approximately the difference between a noble sense of duty and an ignoble fear of punishment; but to this point we shall return anon.

Neither is it correct to identify worry, as a disease, with genuine apprehension. If, on the morrow, a man is to be carved for an ominous growth in his intestines, or if he is to answer a certain number of pointed questions because he was found wiping off a blood-stained baseball bat immediately after his mother-in-law had her empty head bashed in; even if (speaking for my single self) a man has a dental appointment in the morning; such a man will experience a certain unpleasant tremor of apprehension every time he finds himself thinking of the immediate future. As everyone realizes, the most enviable fact about brute animals is that they never suffer this tearing experience about the future. It is God's special gift to the beast that the beast lives purely and wholly in the moment, and this is very just, seeing that the beast has no strict future, anyhow. What a dog does not feel, however, the dog's master certainly does: how often, and with what good reason, will a sleepless man anguish through the secret night, hopelessly wrestling to hold off the sun! It would be bootless, surely, for the Son of God to address an imperative against anxiety to the sweating convict in the death-house as he awaits the dawn of his private d-day. Whatever the vice of worry is, it is not such inescapable apprehension.

Perhaps that word *vice* may help us to an accurate notion of what worry really is. A vice is not an act. A man who gets uproariously drunk every time a Republican is elected president or every time a filly wins the Kentucky Derby may or may not be a sensible man, but he is not a drunkard. So the poor fellow who lies sleepless on the night before he receives the doctor's diagnosis of those paralyzing chest pains is not necessarily a worrier. A vice is a habit, and the vice of worry is the habit of worry.

It should not be difficult for anyone who thinks at all to determine whether or not he is addicted to worry as better men are addicted to drink. There are three small marks, any one of which identifies the professional worrier, although all three are commonly found together.

First, the truly anxious person always worries about the wrong things. He worries about dangers that are relatively remote, like cancer, or dangers which are beyond his control in any event, like war. Here we recognize the busy and not very happy people who wonder whether they bolted the back door, whether the train will be on time, whether it will rain tomorrow, whether they are losing their hair or their figure. These are the exhausting folk

who *always* warn you about the three steps leading down
from the front porch—I *did* miss them once, I recall, and
was none the worse for it—and who not only bundle you
into a car, but lock you in it. These poor souls dread lightning because it is so bright and thunder because it is so
loud. Secondly, the anxious person worries not only about
the wrong things, but about everything. *Ten thousand
forms of death surround us,* old Homer admitted sadly,
and, in this one respect, your true man of worry is indeed
Homeric. I have known a whole family of people who always declined any proposal or rejected any plan or were
opposed to any suggestion as soon as it was made, for they
knew in advance, no matter what the notion was, that no
good could come of it. So the worrier worries about the
past, for how can you ever be sure that all that evil is
forgiven and forgotten; he worries about the present, because did you ever see the world in such a state; he worries
about the future, because you never know, you really can't
be sure, you can only expect that bad will turn to worse.
Thirdly, the anxious man worries disproportionately. A
cold in the head is not pneumonia, a visit to the dentist is
not equivalent to decapitation, a math exam is not the final
judgment (thank God!), but such fine distinctions are lost
on the professional worrier.

The anxiety, therefore, which Christ so roundly condemned in His blundering, well-meaning disciples and
which, we must suppose, He condemns as heartily in us, is
not an act, but a habit, and we ought really to reflect on
that fact, because it is the veritable clue which alone will
lead us to any sort of solution of the acute and exceedingly
prevalent problem of worry among otherwise devout and

intelligent and edifying Christians. In every habit, as the habit becomes more and more deeply ingrained, the elements of rationality and volition—the essential constituents of any free act—tend to decline, and mere mechanical or nervous reaction tends to guide and govern the whole process. The moral theologians caution us that only in a rare case does habit completely supplant volition; but it is emphatically observable that the vice of worry does seem to paralyze both reflection and decision in favor of mere mechanical reaction. Perhaps this paralysis follows from our deplorable refusal to recognize worry as a true moral *vice,* precisely as a different paralysis follows from our steadfast refusal to recognize cheerfulness as a moral *virtue.* In any event, perfectly good and genuinely religious people—and women more often than men—will either insist that they *cannot* stop worrying, or, in the extreme case, will even regard worry as a kind of duty which must be discharged or obligation which must be met. A certain distressed lady used to say, *But someone has got to do the worrying for this family!* True, the lady was not bright; but the point at the moment is that she was not happy, and yet no good was accomplished. So people begin to worry and continue to worry and foster the habit of worry, and they seem never to notice that all the time they are becoming less reasonable and less free. They grow steadily more like madmen and more like slaves, all because of the habit of worry. It is useless to argue that the worriers are sinful, although they are. The point is that they are extraordinarily pitiful. They are not quite human, since reason and volition have become so atrophied, and yet they are nothing so normal and healthy as animals. They are—well, worriers.

Since the chronically anxious do not truly reflect, they never do discover *why* they are anxious, which is to say, they never do find out what worry finally is. In the ultimate analysis, worry is not conscientiousness or a sense of duty or seriousness about life or responsible concern. Worry is fear; and fear of the sort that is stark, craven and debasing. We worry because we are afraid. Why are we afraid? Obviously, because we are surrounded and constantly threatened by fearful realities. True, indeed; and the man is a fool who brays out that he is not afraid of cancer or blindness or sudden, ripping death. Any man with half an eye will fear what seems to be fearful, for any man with half a brain knows that he is not big enough or strong enough to conquer all the flashing or snarling dangers that menace him on every side. So a man of any religion turns to his God for protection against evil. *Dominus, illuminatio mea et salus mea,* he cries: *God, you are the light by which I walk, you are all the security I have. Our Father,* he murmurs, quoting One who should know what He is talking about, *deliver us from evil.* So, and only so, human anxiety dies: the incipient vice of fear is done to death by the newborn virtue of hope. A man stops fearing, not because he is so brave, but because his God is so good.

All this the habitual worrier cannot or will not understand: he simply will not believe that anxiety is nothing but base, cowardly fear which flows from a sheer lack of confidence in God. The worrier does not believe this because he does not think it, and he does not think it because he does not think. Since he does not think, the anxious person is never ashamed of what is shameful; he is not ashamed of his anxiety.

Christ our good Lord was clear enough on this subject, heaven knows. In one of His most eloquent and tender passages He begged us all not to be anxious: *Ne solliciti sitis, Do not worry.* And by way of illustration our Savior chose the very two things which, one would say, a reasonable man has *got* to be anxious about: what he will wear and what he will eat. Our Lord pointed to the bright field-lilies which were blooming at His feet and to the downy fatness of the birds that skimmed and swooped through the air, and asked what is, for any man of faith in God, the unanswerable question: If your Father so clothes these and so feeds these, will He fail to do as much for you, who mean so much more to Him than all of these together? *Do not fret, then,* our Savior concluded.

So that day in the boat Christ really did maul His beloved friends with not a few hard words. In spite of all He had said on that other occasion, and, no doubt, on many other occasions, the disciples were still anxious, and they were still anxious about getting enough to eat. Our Savior clearly regards their anxiety as an affront, He brands their worry as a lapse from the standard of moral behavior He had set for them. He scolds them in measured terms, for they *must*—as they believe in Him—learn not to worry.

Two thousand years have passed, and yet we do not understand our Lord on the subject of worry. It is strange, indeed, and very sad. How many generations there have been of glowing lilies and plump robins, and the words of Christ, exactly as He foretold, have not passed away, and yet the end result of the whole process is, in too many cases, just a new generation of worriers, a new disorganized army of people who are still convinced that there won't be enough for all of us to eat, or, if there is, that it will give us indigestion. The worriers, like the poor, will be with us always, apparently. But there is no beatitude for the worriers; only more worry.

"Lord, he said, have pity on my son . . . I brought him here to thy
disciples, but they have not been able to cure him."

MATTHEW 17:14-15

XII

THE FATHER OF THE LUNATIC BOY

In the Catholic Church clergy and laity wear different uniforms, but they
are all on the same team. So of course there has got to be team-work.

Anyone who is at all interested in Jesus of Nazareth, and especially anyone who in any sense loves the Son of Mary, must at some time or other have envied the twelve Apostles. About the individual members of this uniquely privileged group we don't know very much, for only Peter and John, and, to a lesser degree, unhappy Judas, emerge as clearly defined personalities in the Gospel story. What we do know is that, of all men in all human history, this even dozen spent the better part of three years in close and apparently steady companionship with the Savior of all the world. The fact alone is warrant enough for our envy, but perhaps we also envy the Twelve by reason of a fairly erroneous inference which we almost instinctively draw from the fact. We tend to assume that because our Lord's disciples were actually with Him, they had a serene and tranquil and happy time of it: their troubles were few, and the complete, incarnate Answer to their problems was always at hand. There is a grain of truth in such an idea, but not much more than a grain. The rest of the story is that the Apostolic College, like any other college, ran into some whacking big troubles which were by no means strictly academic, and the Gospel accounts hint pretty broadly that the disciples were not always altogether happy about the way their well loved Master treated them in their difficulties. A striking instance of Apostles mired deep in trouble is recorded by all three Synoptics, as Matthew, Mark, and Luke are called in separation from John.

On the morning after that utterly unique event, the Transfiguration, our Savior and the three privileged witnesses of what Peter afterward called *the splendor that dazzles human eyes* came slowly down from Thabor to rejoin the rest of the Apostles. Matthew and Mark tell us something of the quiet conversation that took place during that reluctant descent from ecstasy to commonplace existence, and a certain aura of wonder and awe seems to cling to the simple words and sentences even as we read them now. And immediately the lovely spell of Thabor is shattered by a babel of raucous, angry voices and the pounding of running feet. An excited, swirling crowd of people engulfs our Savior and His three special friends; with somewhat more dignity half a dozen complacent Scribes, looking like cats full of canaries, make their way through the crowd; and with steps that seem to drag, nine morose and smouldering disciples gradually filter into the immediate vicinity of our Lord. By that time, however, a very ordinary-looking man has placed himself before Christ, and with considerable vehemence is pouring out what we would correctly term a tale of woe.

It was indeed a tale of woe—like so many human stories.

The man was the father of an only child, a son, and the boy was in truly desperate and pitiful case. He was a masochistic psychotic; he was epileptic; he was deaf and dumb; he was possessed by an unclean spirit. As far as external indications go, every priest and doctor, and many another, too, has seen such dreadfully afflicted children. They are not only heartrending, but are what children should never be, positively frightening; for they seem more animal than human. Apparently, while the poor man talked, the tormented boy was being held apart—for he clearly required restraint—by some of those good-hearted people who always appear on the stage of human sorrow, ready to lend a hand with the most distasteful tasks on the most painful occasions. The distracted father pours out the sad case history of his boy, and as we listen, we can readily imagine the worried days and endless, sleepless nights the poor man has passed trying to be a true father to a half-human child. The boy was a suicidal maniac; he had tried repeatedly to drown himself, and, incredibly, even to burn himself to death. Then, as the crestfallen disciples shuffled their feet and muttered and looked away, the father of the psychotic cried out to our Lord his bitter disappointment: *I brought him here to Thy disciples . . . I entreated . . . but they were powerless . . . they have not been able to cure him.*

Such, then, was the humiliating experience of nine Apostles while the three fortunate ones were revelling in the shining glory of the Transfiguration. A father had brought his possessed son to be cured by our Lord. In the absence of the Master, the man appealed to the disciples to help him. It must be remembered that this precise

supernatural power over demons had previously been specifically granted by our Savior to His disciples when He
had sent them out on their first missionary tour. So the
Apostles not unreasonably undertook the exorcism of the
frantic child; and they met with unqualified failure. To
add to their frustration, a number of our Lord's faithful
enemies were witnesses of the whole miserable performance, and it is easy to imagine what capital these better-
educated Scribes made of the apostolic failure. By the
time our Lord appeared, that had taken place which
usually occurs in such tangled and human affairs: the
afflicted boy and his heartbroken father had been shoved
into the background, and center stage was now occupied
by a wrathful and recriminatory theological debate, Apostles versus Scribes, with the Scribes well out in front.

Our Savior's first reaction on this occasion was curious.
He uttered a vigorous protest against the lack of faith on
the part of *this misguided, perverse generation,* but He
certainly was not addressing the father of the sick boy, for
He spoke in the plural. It seems doubtful that such a
resounding rebuke should be directed at the already hu-
miliated disciples, especially in view of the mild and
matter-of-fact explanation of the failure which our Lord
subsequently provided. Our Savior was apparently speaking to and of the entire crowd which milled about Him,
typical as it was of the people who had already begun to
reject Him in Galilee and of those in slick Judea who never
had in any sense accepted Him for what He was. Our
Lord ordered the afflicted boy to be brought to Him. For
our enlightenment, rather than His own, He questioned
the father further about the child's affliction. Then, as in

all but a few miracles, came His uncompromising demand for absolute and entire interior faith in Him. The anguished father broke down completely, and, in a touching, tearful and truthful prayer, offered to Christ the best that was in him: *Lord, I do believe; succor my unbelief.* Christ Jesus never spurns the best a man has to offer, and He immediately ordered the evil spirit out of the boy. The poor child flew into a wild and ghastly convulsion; we may picture the horrified crowd backing away to make a small circle around Jesus and the threshing, palpitating, gagging, contorted boy. Then suddenly the child lay still and white on the ground. In the frightened silence someone said what everyone was thinking: "He's dead." Our Savior bent over and took the boy by the hand. The child arose, quiet and clear-eyed and a little surprised. Perhaps he looked about him, caught his father's eye, and smiled. Surely, before he turned away to his father's arms, he looked for a long, wondering, loving moment into the blessed face that kings and non-kings would have given so much to see.

So much for the exciting event of the psychotic boy. But once again, it is neither the boy nor his illness nor his cure nor our Savior's unfailing kindness that makes for our present purpose. We are interested now only in the father of the possessed boy, and we are concerned with only one fact about him: the fact that he complained about our Lord's disciples. Perhaps we may see in this small detail the symbol and prototype of whatever difficulty or tension may exist today between clergy and laity in the world of the Catholic Church.

It must be obvious to every fair-minded person that the general relationship between the Catholic priest and the

Catholic people today is a cordial, close and happy one. To begin with, there is a very great deal of actual personal contact between priests and people in the routine functioning of the Catholic Church. The constant obligation of Sunday Mass, the modern relative frequency of confession and Holy Communion, Baptisms, First Communions, Confirmations, the education of the children, sickness, death in the family, parish and diocesan organizations, public novenas, and, where the dour, gimlet-eyed spiritual descendants of Calvin and John Knox permit, Bingo—all these serve to keep priest and people in steady and intimate association. Whatever else the priest and the Catholic may be to one another, they are not strangers. Next, the deep and ancient respect, amounting to veneration, of the Catholic laity for the priesthood as a sacred and truly divine institution exists today almost unimpaired, and it is (if I may say so) a thing wholly distinct from the attitude of the average Protestant toward the man, officially not a whit different from himself, who by some extrinsic determination happens to be his minister. Anyone who has ever attended a Catholic ordination or First Mass knows perfectly well that he has witnessed in the universal reaction of the laity present a reality far more genuine than a mere sentimental religious orgy. This reverence survives to a marked degree even in the routine dealings of people with the priest, although that fine old title, "Your Reverence," has gone the way of all splendid external manners. Furthermore, it not infrequently happens that our people entertain for their priests not only a profound respect, but a most genuine and artless and unashamed affection. Indeed, the second greatest danger for the young priest is the busy, gossiping tongues of people who want him to be super-human; the greatest danger is the love of people who want him to be much too human. Still, one of the sweetest small experiences of the priest is the unabashed love he receives from Catholic children, and there are whole slathers of Catholic people who, in this lovely sense, never do grow up. Finally, the Catholic priest, despite all his very human failings, does invariably give to the sons and daughters of Holy Mother Church a lifetime of devoted, unsparing labor and generally efficient service.

So we may assert, without a tinge of conventional, merely verbal optimism, that, in general, the current situation of clergy and laity in the Catholic Church is a deal more than just satisfactory. However, this ointment of holy harmony is not without its flies. We think it will do no harm to put the flies, as well as the ointment, under the microscope.

Whatever clergy-laity problem there is might best be approached by noting a basic, significant and inevitable change that has taken place in that relationship in the last one hundred and especially the last fifty years.

The second half of the nineteenth century was the age of declining Victorianism, of booming industrialism, of the most naive scientific pretension. It was likewise an era of vast emigration from Europe, and especially from Catholic Europe, to the United States. As might be expected, those huge, successive waves of emigration and immigration did not commonly sweep people from European castles and manors and baronial estates to the farms and shops and factories of youthful, lusty America. The bulk of the people who washed up on these shores were penniless peasants (the word is used in the widest sense) who came to America in the simple and understandable hope of regularly getting enough to eat.

Now peasants are universally and correctly regarded as possessing a wealth of common sense, that being the only wealth they have, and a goodly number of the honest folk who found their way to the glittering New World had had the good sense not to learn to read or write, much less fiddle or flirt with higher forms of education. When the Catholic section of this uprooted peasantry gradually settled down in Boston and Baltimore and Philadelphia and New York and all the feasible places north and west, though not much south, of these cities, the person to whom they immediately and instinctively turned for help in difficulties was their priest.

Two points are here strictly to be noted. First, this transplanted, largely illiterate Catholic peasantry turned to the priest in *all*, again underscore *all*, their problems and doubts and troubles. The priest read letters and wrote answers to them; he secured jobs; he got men out of jail, and, with somewhat more difficulty, out of saloons, and afterwards rammed down their throats the temperance pledge as a chaser for too much whiskey; he made the necessary arrangements when enough dollars had been painfully saved and scraped together to make sufficient pounds to fetch cousin Katey, bless her heart, out here from the Old Country. It was the priest who explained to his shabby but shrewd and attentive flock just what was in the newspapers that many of them couldn't read, and, by a most natural progression, it was the good Father who told his poor children whom to vote for and what to vote against, for he was the lad who knew best of all what side their bread was buttered on.

As it happened—and this is the second point here to be noted—the typical American priest of that seething, exciting, dawn-like era was not American at all, nor was he, in any technical sense, either a saint or a scholar or a gentleman. He was commonly a beefy, heavy-handed, hardheaded, iron-lunged Irishman or German or Italian or Pole who might have been somewhat bibulous, and who might even have left his native land and native diocese in something of a hurry. The man was what he was; but, above all else, he was truly a priest, he was a worker, he was crushingly decisive, he was fearless, he was devoted to his ragged, underprivileged people. He was or may not have been a hero, but he was just what the moment and the Church and the people called for. Is it any wonder, then, that there grew up around the American parish priest a strong habit and tradition and atmosphere of absolute authoritarianism in all his dealings with the laity? Can any honest observer of human affairs pretend to be surprised that for the American Catholic people of past generations the word of the priest was law, even though Father Gilhooly's word frequently extended to matter that lay far outside the widest imaginable boundaries of the Apostles' Creed?

Well, the generations multiplied, as generations will. The sons and daughters (and there were plenty of them, God be praised) of the Catholic immigrant peasants were hounded and hustled off to school to learn their a-b-c's, and the foxy Jesuits and the holy nuns started high schools and colleges for Catholic boys and Catholic girls. The

Polish laborer's son opened an office as a certified public accountant, the Italian barber's oldest boy became a doctor and a surgeon, the German butcher's smart little girls grew into starched, crisp nurses and competent teachers, the Irish grocer's youngest lawyer-son, supported originally only by the Holy Name Society, was finally elected mayor of the growing town. And all these and all like them sent their burgeoning sons and daughters to the best schools the nation afforded. Now, in this middle of the twentieth century, now in the age of jet-planes and frozen foods and atomic energy, where and how do the Catholic descendants of the illiterate immigrant peasants stand in relation to the spiritual descendants of roaring old Father Gilhooly and Father Bogatski and Father Himmelreicher, gone these many long years to their rich reward?

Obviously, the relationship between priest and people has changed. We insist that the change is not an essential one, but only a variation in accidental or incidental characteristics. The change may be for the better, it may be for the worse, but there it is. The pastor need no longer explain to his flock what is printed in the newspapers, for they could probably give him lessons from *Time*, *Life*, and the *Ladies Home Journal*. Father will no longer suggest from the pulpit that a vote for the Democratic party is a vote for God as well as country—not, that is, unless he is content to have episcopal thunder crashing in his ears. The priest today will speak most guardedly of evolution, nuclear physics, biochemistry, the theory of relativity, economics, history and the Church-State question, for it's a rare congregation that will not be tolerably informed on all these matters and that will not contain a couple of professional experts on any one of them. In a word, the contemporary priest may not, at risk of folly, talk down to his people, he will not for a moment pose as an encyclopedia just because he is a priest, he need not any longer make all the decisions that now securely rest with his flock. In a very real if limited sense, the majority of the sons and daughters of the Catholic Church in America are now big boys and girls, and must be regarded and treated as such. All this is generally well understood by both priests and people; nevertheless, the new relationship has generated certain stresses and strains.

On the part of the Catholic laity, the fundamental contemporary fault in this matter is the pronounced and growing tendency to reduce the true stature and worth and position of the priest by regarding him as just another public servant. In this view, the local pastor and his assistants are professional social workers of a sort, whose salaries are being paid by the people, whose qualifications are estimated and measured according to strictly natural and visible standards, and whose life, by and large, is as soft and lush and cushy as a human life can be. Since Father is being supported by the people, his primary function is to give good service, hour for dollar, in return for his keep, the nature of the good service depending, of course, on the personal tastes and opinions of the individual parishioner. Since Father is more or less a professional social worker, he ought to have advanced professional knowledge of modern social service. Also of contemporary economics. Also of the latest trends in chemistry, physics and biology. Also of finance and business procedure. Also of geo-politics. Also of basic medicine and civil law. Also of psychiatry. Naturally, also, he should possess a polished, mundane mode of speech and action, he ought to have a slick bedside manner, he simply must be a first-rate public speaker. Above all, the priest ought to be instantly available, when I want him, the way I want him, and ready with what I want of him. After all, doesn't he have a nicer life than any of us?

What emerges most clearly in this view of the Catholic priest is something that is not in it at all. It is the supernatural. In all the feverish, demanding talk and thought of service, money, ease and psychiatry we hear not a word about—for example—the Holy Sacrifice of the Mass. Yet a priest's first task, according to no less an authority than St. Paul, is to say Mass. Whether anyone wants it or not. Whether anyone is there or not. The Holy Sacrifice is here used simply as a concrete example of a whole world of reality which, both for the priest and for the people in their relation to him, is the true world of reality. For the truth is that Father McGillicuddy is *not* a social worker. He is a priest. It is a pity that when people complain of the pastor's sermon at Mass they do not at all notice that the pastor did say Mass. And they do not seem to suspect that he probably offered the Mass for them.

On the part of the contemporary priest, the fundamental fault, I venture to suggest, is not at all any of those sensational and lamentable failures that occasionally occur in the ranks of the Catholic clergy. The real fault is a certain lack of zeal, and zeal is only another and inferior word for love of people. The problem here mentioned (and more, at the moment, we will not attempt) is extremely complex, for it is both spiritual and psychological, and would require a detailed and delicate discussion that would now be out of place. Supposing, however, a certain truth in our contention, such a failure in downright zeal or authentic love of those people, frequently most naturally unattractive, who are entrusted to our care would be the adequate explanation of those unlovely traits in us priests which the faithful find most offensive and most disappointing: impatience, hardness, lack of sympathy, laziness, love of ease and comfort and money. It is the personal problem of every earnest priest to keep alive, and as far as may be, truly flaming, the pentecostal zeal which did burn in his heart on the morning of his ordination.

The father of the epileptic boy was probably not the first simple and unhappy man to be disappointed in the disciples of Christ our Lord. He was not the last. Perhaps priests will always disappoint our Lord's people a little, as they undoubtedly disappoint Him, at times more than a little. Still, the faithful could at least see to it that they are not disappointed in their priests for all the wrong reasons. We can all help and truly serve one another, if we will just love one another, supernaturally, in Christ Jesus.

"Here there was a woman who . . . was bent down, and could not lift her head straight."

LUKE 13:11

XIII

THE DEFORMED WOMAN

The poor little lady who was so bent over *had* to keep looking at the ground; but do we?

St. Luke, the human author of the third Gospel and Paul's well-loved doctor, was also that fascinating and disturbing thing, an artist; for he was a truly literary man. It may be questioned whether anyone has ever told an exciting story more excitingly than did Luke in the Acts of the Apostles. Now a truly literary man, like any genuine artist, is subject to a certain type of indifference or disinterest which baffles and at times infuriates your conscientious scientist, who can only regard such innocent indifference as shoddy carelessness. St. Luke's indifference extends chiefly to those two details—interesting, undoubtedly, yet only details—which modern journalism has taught us to prize as the true heart of any matter: even more than the other Evangelists, Luke, happy man, doesn't care about time and place. So it happens that the entire middle portion of the third Gospel, some nine chapters out of twenty-four, which enriches us with such treasures as the healing of the ten lepers, the domestic difference between Martha and Mary and that pearl of our Lord's parables, the story of the

Prodigal Son, has knocked years off the lives of Scripture scholars and Gospel harmonizers. Luke says that things happened, but he doesn't say when. He tells, unforgettably, what our Lord did and said, but he rarely tells where. At one point (toward the beginning of his thirteenth chapter) Luke remarks absent-mindedly that the event he is about to narrate took place in a synagogue on the Sabbath day, and the sorely tried Scripture people have pounced hungrily on that casual statement. From the close of our Savior's ministry in Galilee in the early part of His last mortal autumn until His death in Jerusalem the following spring, this verse in Luke makes the only reference to preaching in any synagogue. The incident which occurred is a brief and quite simple one, but it possesses certain notable details. Above all, it introduces us to a little lady who may prove a profitable acquaintance.

The running battle between our divine Savior, on the one hand, and His professional Jewish enemies, usually designated as the Scribes and Pharisees, on the other, had taken its rise at the first Passover of our Lord's public life, when He had outraged the intrenched legal and ecclesiastical authorities by the sensational cleansing of the Temple; but the conflict had taken its form, so to speak, about a year later, possibly at the second Passover, when our Savior had performed a striking miracle on the Sabbath day. That cure of the long-paralyzed man at the Probatic Pool must have been the only one of our Lord's miracles which really suited His enemies, for at once they perceived that finally they had some sort of weapon to bludgeon Him with. Touchy to the point of madness were the Jewish teachers on the subject of the sacred Sabbath. No less than thirty-nine different types of work were specifically forbidden on the Lord's day, ranging from sowing and plowing to clapping the hands or carrying a weight of food equivalent to the weight of a dried fig. From the time, therefore, of this first Sabbath miracle the question of the Sabbath observance became the steady bone of contention between our Savior and the Jews. The argument flames again in the event which now concerns us from Luke's thirteenth chapter.

Our Savior, on this Sabbath morning, had acted as guest preacher in this particular synagogue, in accordance with the Jewish custom of inviting itinerant rabbis to give the instruction which, in the morning service, followed the reading from Scripture. Curiously, it is Luke who records both the first and the last synagogue sermons of our Lord; but though he gives us the text and a digest of our Savior's remarks on the first occasion, there is no hint as to what Jesus said in this last synagogue appearance. At any rate, when the sermon ended, our Lord did not at once return to a place among the worshippers on the men's side of the synagogue. He continued to stand on the reader's platform, His eyes fixed on someone who stood on the women's side. *He called her to Him,* says St. Luke; and timidly the little and perhaps old lady came slowly forward.

There is a certain amount of discussion both as to what, exactly, this lady's physical disability was, and what was the cause of it. Luke the doctor is here exasperatingly vague: the woman *had a spirit of infirmity.* But perhaps the Evangelist is writing like any conscientious and honest doctor; perhaps he did not *know* what the illness was. On two points, however, Luke is lucid: the lady had been afflicted for eighteen years, or since our Lord had been a boy of fourteen; and she was now bent over, so that she could not lift her head erect. We have all seen unfortunate afflictions of this sort, and we all know the unhappy, shrunken, wizened and peering impression they make on the observer. So the little bent lady stood before Christ, staring, willy-nilly, at His feet.

What followed was rapid, and remarkably without elaborate ceremony or fanfare. This is one of those rare instances where our Lord asked not the slightest token of faith before He performed a wonder. We can only conclude that by His divine knowledge He knew the woman's interior dispositions to be satisfactory. He said simply, as one who merely states a fact, *Woman, thou art rid of thy infirmity*. He extended His hands and rested them upon the bowed head. As He withdrew His hands, the little lady simply straightened up, lifted her head, and looked—who shall say with what shining eyes and trembling lips and sudden tears?—into the most beautiful and blessed of all faces.

The sequel to this kindly, unsolicited marvel borders on the incredible, but it certainly delineates the shockingly gross and dehumanized mentality with which Christ had to cope during His public life.

Each Jewish synagogue possessed a roster of officials, few or none of whom were priests, and prominent among whom was the *archisynagogus* or head of the synagogue. The head of the synagogue was not really a governing officer, but discharged a very limited part of the duties of a modern pastor: he was responsible for the proper condition of the building, and for the proper conduct of religious services. In the present instance the *archisynagogus* apparently bustled forward to the place on the reader's platform which our Lord had just vacated, and delivered himself of an indignant imperative which, for pure, unfeeling, rock-ribbed imbecility, would be hard to match. He said: *You have six days on which work is allowed; you should come and be healed on those days, not on the Sabbath.* The pronouncement, apart from its blind malevolence, is difficult to analyze. The poor bent lady had surely not come to the morning synagogue service with the faintest expectation of being literally straightened out, and even so, her coming could not possibly be classified as work. If anyone had done anything remotely resembling the mad rabbinic idea of work it was our Lord when He placed His hands on the woman's head. But of course the *archisynagogus* had not the hardihood to challenge our Savior directly, so, after the manner of his kind, he spat his stupid venom at those who could not possibly retaliate. It is with satisfaction that we read the remainder of Luke's stirring narrative. The icy voice of Christ cracked like a whip through that synagogue. He employed a plural vocative, for He was speaking not only to the contemptible *archisynagogus*, but to all his sort. As usual, our Savior unhesitatingly applies the right word to the right people: *What, you hypocrites! Is there any one of you that will not untie his ox or his ass from the stall and take them down to water, when it is the Sabbath? And here is this daughter of Abraham, whom Satan had kept bound these eighteen years past; was it wrong that she should be delivered on the Sabbath day from bonds like these?* Our blessed Lord's argument is His favorite one of *a fortiori* comparison. Typically, the canny Pharisees readily allowed on the Lord's day the labor of caring for livestock, not, we may be sure, out of any feeling for the cattle, but with tender regard for the financial investment which cattle represented. Our Savior simply argues that it ought to be licit to do on a supernatural level for a woman what you may properly do on a natural level for an animal. In effect, Jesus is arguing that a human being is more important than a jackass; which would seem to be a fairly solid and defensible contention. Luke's closing observation is exactly what we wish to hear: *All His adversaries were put to shame by this saying of His, and the whole multitude rejoiced over the marvellous works He did.*

What might possibly be the significance of the little bent woman, the *mulier inclinata* whom St. Gregory the Great gently describes as *mulier curva,* the curved or somewhat crooked lady? What might be her meaning for us, especially in her striking juxtaposition to the *archisynagogus fatuus,* the fat-head of the synagogue? We mildly suggest that the little crooked lady, whom our loving Lord healed, as it were, so handily, accurately symbolizes in her bent body what the *archisynagogus* was suffering from in his deformed soul. The head of the synagogue was interiorly bent over, he was deformed, he was imprisoned, he was cabined and cribbed and confined, by a serious soul-malady. He was afflicted with smallness. This is by no means the littleness which, by divine command, we are to imitate in children. This is the smallness which is narrowness. In a variety of forms, the mean little virus attacks many a man and woman who would like to lead a truly Christian life.

A primary symptom of smallness as a disease of the spirit is the habitual frame of mind which we term extreme legalism.

Religious legalism in our day is the legitimate but ill-favored child of an unhappy marriage between Pharisaism (which comes down to us through the unquestionable Judaic stream in Christianity) and Puritanism (the end result of Calvinism plus Oliver Cromwell plus that benighted old tub, the *Mayflower*). Religious legalists are of two sorts, the first of which, speaking very broadly, is Protestant, and the second, Catholic.

The first kind of religious legalist values law for this above all else, that it can effectively prevent people from enjoying themselves. Here we meet, however unwillingly, the strange people who engineered and foisted upon the entire nation the monstrosity of Prohibition. Here we encounter the less articulate but equally unappetizing folk who feel sure that the tobacco leaf was first and secretly planted by Satan both in Paradise and in the American South immediately after the fall of man, in flagrant violation of the everlasting divine decree which was clearly tacked up on every tree in Eden, *No Smoking*.

Here, too, we sadly come up against the anti-Bingo crusaders. There exists in this big, broad country of ours—and of course this country, like our Lord's net let down into the sea, is big enough to contain all kinds of queer fish—a certain type of Evangelical (he is in no sense a divine) who is haunted and obsessed by a certain type of mental image. As a weaker and much better man might be tormented with

interior visions of primal paroxysms of hot and sweaty lust,
so this Evangelical is tortured by the goading, salty phan-
tasm of a hall full of elderly ladies sitting in orderly rows
before Bingo cards and listening silently to the voluptuous
chanting of the man who is calling the numbers. These nice
old ladies come together with a double intent: first, they desire with a kind of primeval innocence to escape for a brief
evening from the tasks and troubles of domesticity; secondly—or does this come first?—they assemble in the fond
hope of winning ten dollars with which they might for
once buy a new hat without being beholden to their
grumpy lords and masters. Such is the diabolical vision
which whips some ministers of the Gospel into furies of
declamation, hustles them before legislatures and con-
vinces them that the Catholic Church, which cherishes a
tolerant affection for Bingo and especially for the profits
from Bingo, is indeed the naughty lady who is so roundly
denounced in the Apocalypse. Behold the very model of
the contemporary *archisynagogus*, who no longer screams
because people come to church on Sunday in order to be
cured, but because people go to the church hall on one
night of the week in order to have fun!

The second type of religious legalist is not much more
lovable than the first, but he is apt to be considerably more
intelligent. This is the man who labors under either a con-
genital or somehow acquired intellectual imbalance: his
mind is legal. Such a person—almost never a woman, by
the way—is inclined, by the whole force and tendency of
his temperament, not so much to action as to the measure-
ment of action, precisely as another person is not interested
in action at all, but in abstract speculation or concrete

beauty. The truly legal man does not really ask about any deed *Is it profitable?* or *Is it exalted?* or *Is it momentous?*; immediately and instinctively he questions, *Does this act wholly conform to a certain standard or norm?* It goes without saying that such men have their uses, and very noble uses, in a human family which numbers among its deepest desires an indefatigable hankering for anarchy. But the legal mind, like every other type of mind, suffers from itself. Its recurrent and really ominous temptation is to value law, not for what it does or what it means to do, not for the sake of the benevolent lawmaker or the simple humans who will gain by it, but simply and purely for its own sake. In his last and worst state the legalist does not care a hoot for either the lawmaker or the law-bound or the very purpose of the law. He just loves the law. It is the old story: one way or another, we all tend to promote a means to the much more exalted status of an end.

In the area of religion or the supernatural, this second type of legalist may well become a hard and angular and fiercely critical person. If he does not lack mercy he will lack a certain tone or warmth or even tenderness which is such a notable and moving element in God's mercy, as witness the parable of the Prodigal Son. Above all, our religious legalist will lack both tolerance and humor. The laborious and uncertain adjustment of the children of Adam to any fairly permanent standard is not primarily comic, because there is question of a serious moral obligation to conform to a seriously binding norm; but if the adjustment is not essentially comic it is not mechanical, either, but simply human, and therefore ought to be regarded humanely. Human behavior is in great part a disorderly clutter of loose ends, unfinished business, woeful dereliction, astonishing and sometimes absurd heroism, lethargy, sudden energy, latecoming and unanswered letters. Such an unholy medley or stew may be distressing to precise and orderly souls, but such has pretty much been the state of human affairs since the Fall, and such it is going to remain. As it was in the beginning, is now and almost ever shall be, but a world with an end, amen, and thank God for that, anyhow. The religious legalist will and frequently must keep his eye on the law and the observance of it, but let him keep the other eye—whichever one has the better vision—fixed firmly and as lovingly as may be, not on things at all, but on persons: the sublime and most merciful Persons of God, the supreme Lawmaker, and the bumbling human persons who find it so very difficult to believe with any degree of conviction that God is not merely a legislator but a loving Father who really does know what is best for His children. Religious legalists do not need more learning or precision. They need pity. That is to say, they need more love. They probably pray a good deal to the Holy Spirit, but they keep asking for the wrong thing.

Legalism is not the only symptom or result of smallness of soul. Everyone knows that many a man will endure major suffering with a deal more fortitude than he will show in putting up with minor irritations, but there is a limit to this sort of thing, too. It is the hopeless conviction of this writer, a conviction based primarily on years of feeble struggling with himself, that one of the most surprising and really notable faults in priests and professional religious as distinct from devout layfolk is this

same extreme sensitivity to and preoccupation with petty
annoyances.

Perhaps we priests and religious are, in a certain sense,
inevitably spoiled, either because our training involves so
much necessary insistence on small details of observance
and behavior, or because—thanks to poverty and chastity
and, it may be, even to obedience—we frequently pass
through whole periods in our lives without encountering a
single trouble of any magnitude. Whatever the explanation, I, for one, find myself absurdly and ridiculously upset
by too much heat in summer and too little heat in coffee,
by a fly in my study and a mosquito in my bedroom,* by
a passing cold in the head, by two days of steady rain, by
the elusive people who are always last into the chapel and
first out of it, by the wretched women who gabble when I
want to listen to a concert or try to preach a sermon. There
isn't a single item in this nugatory catalogue, or among the
countless additions that could be made to it, which is
worth a particular damn; but many a hearty damn have I
interiorly and not always just interiorly expended on what
Shakespeare calls "such small deer."

The intention of the writer at this point is not to make
a general confession in print, diverting as that might be.
He would merely like to remark with a certain amount of
acidity that he does not feel specially isolated in his fum-
ing and preposterous response to petty vexations. He is
indeed sorry in this matter, but he is by no means unique.
The average priest or religious, together with many a sin-

* This is said purely for effect. I have only one room, so the fly and the
mosquito are really together. They just work different hours. Sometimes
there are moths, too.

cere Christian layman, would probably make a superb and unhesitating martyr in a flaming hour of persecution. The trouble, however, with the recurrent martyrdom of daily existence is that it calls for so much more than a single stroke of virtue. *Non vi, sed saepe cadendo,* runs an old Latin tag, which might be rendered, if not translated, thus: *A thousand tiny self-denials will make as bright and true and crimson a martyr as the slash of any sword.*

There is a spaciousness, a glad, generous bigness, about both the gorgeous world of matter which surrounds us and the noble world of the spirit to which we are called, that makes a thinking man more ashamed of smallness than of a greater vice. Gentle reader, we need not pretend, you and I, that we are all bad; but isn't it true that even in our badness, whatever it is, we would like to perceive a certain bigness? The religious legalist and the person who lies at the mercy of every insolent trifle are not evil men. They *are* small men, bent and curved and crippled men. They should think about the little bent lady in the synagogue, and pray the great-hearted Christ to do for them what he did for the little lady: to straighten them up, and so straighten them out.

Jesus loved Martha, and her sister . . .

JOHN 11:5

XIV

MARY AND MARTHA

There's a whole army of women in this miry world who will never be women of distinction. They lack glamor, you see.

It is unfortunate that we cannot, without a sense of discomfort, talk with simplicity about the women in our Lord's life, because that innocent set of words has come to have an ugly significance which can have nothing to do with the sacred Person of the Incarnate Word. As a matter of fact, there were many women in our Savior's life, some of them most wonderfully good, some of them quite strikingly bad. What is really significant, however, is this: no woman met Christ without taking a turn for the better. The same cannot be said of the men; it is not true of Caiphas or Annas or Pilate or the Pharisees or unhappy Judas. It has long been widely noticed and remarked that no woman played an abetting part in the passion and execution of our Savior.

At the town of Bethany, which was situated on the eastern slope of the Mount of Olives at a distance of about two miles from Jerusalem, there lived a pair of women who figure prominently in the Gospel narrative as devoted friends of Christ our Lord. The names of these two ladies

were Martha and Mary, and we know a surprising lot about
them.

To begin with, Martha and Mary were sisters. They be-
longed to a family which strikes the attentive reader of the
Gospels as having been prominent and well-to-do. One
notes, for example, the place of residence. Travellers tell
us that Bethany today is a handful of huts built among
ruins, but the Bethany of our Lord's day would surely have
ranked as a choice and desirable Jerusalem suburb. It was
within easy distance of the Jewish world-center, yet it was
sheltered and secluded by the sloping bulk of the Mount
of Olives, and it enjoyed a sweeping view of Jordan-plain
even to the Dead Sea. Such a locality would hardly have
been a slums. Moreover, all the details surrounding the
sensational miracle which was granted this family, together
with the ominous sequel to the miracle, suggest that the
family was prominent, influential and affluent. The third
known member of the household was the celebrated
Lazarus.

Mary and Martha are mentioned together on three distinct occasions in the Gospel narratives, and, in view of
the notorious and tantalizing brevity of the four Evangelists, this mere fact commands attention. St. Luke tells us
at the end of his tenth chapter that on our Savior's final
journey from Galilee to Jerusalem He was entertained in
the home of Martha and Mary. However, the incident
which Luke recounts in this connection makes it all but
infallibly certain that this visit by our Lord was by no
means the first of its kind. Women of any taste would
rather die than involve a new and distinguished guest in a
family dispute, but good women will unhesitatingly do

exactly that in the case of a familiar, frequent and trusted visitor. Our Savior, of course, did not allow Himself to be drawn into anything so explosive as an earnest family difference; He is never more charming or more tactful than He was on this occasion. How marvelous is the Incarnate Word!

Very different and dark is the next occasion on which we meet the Bethany family. This chronicle is St. John's, and it is one of those outstanding and circumstantial narratives that could not possibly be the work of anyone but an eye-witness, which is exactly what John was to the whole chain of events. His story is this.

In the final stage of His public life, our blessed Savior, meticulously following the timetable of redemption that had been eternally drawn up in the timeless councils of the glorious Trinity, retired once more from the menacing and supercharged atmosphere of Jerusalem and Judea to the comparative safety of Perea beyond the Jordan. There our Redeemer devoted Himself busily but quietly to the instruction of people and the final formation of the Apostles. One day there arrived from Judea a messenger; he may have been a household servant or slave from the family of Bethany. His message was brief but endlessly eloquent: *Lord, he whom Thou lovest lies here sick.* If we knew nothing more about Martha and Mary than that they had addressed this single sentence to Christ, we would know enough for our deepest admiration. The message is clear, reverent, humble, trustful and so full of love. Our Savior probably nodded, and gravely thanked the courier. Two days passed. We may surmise that John, at least, noted this baffling lapse of precious time with astonishment and perhaps something like pain, for many years later, as in old age he writes the fourth Gospel, he remembers distinctly those forty-eight hours. At last, after one of His most delightful recorded dialogues with His Apostles, our Lord led the way back to Bethany.

All that followed is set down in John's eleventh chapter with unforgettable vividness, and every detail speaks of the utter devotion of two good women both to their brother and their Lord. The independent and unrehearsed and heartbroken cry of both the sisters to Christ was identical: *Lord, if Thou hadst been here, my brother would not have died.* Everything that Martha does and says is characteristic. She goes first and unobtrusively to meet Jesus, perhaps hoping to soften the meeting between Him and her sister. Torn as she is with grief, she speaks to our Lord with clarity and coherence, and then returns to summon Mary in her typically tactful and quiet way. At the climactic moment, when our Savior gives the order to open the tomb, it is Martha who instinctively expresses the practical objection. As for Mary, St. John's careful narrative somehow suggests in her a kind of extremity of woeful anguish for her dead brother. It is her tears which John recalls, as he recalls Martha's words. The entire event makes a story of deep love: the love of Mary and Martha for our Savior, His love for them and Lazarus (only on this and one other occasion does Christ weep in the four Gospels); above all, we read here of the devoted love of two sisters for a brother.

We last see Mary and Martha as a pair on the last Saturday night of our Lord's life, at the banquet given Him in Bethany at the home of that mysterious Simon who apparently had been a leper and who quite possibly had been cured by our Savior. Again the parts played by the sisters are characteristic: Martha waited on Christ as He sat at table, and Mary knelt at His feet, anointing them, near as they were to the end of mortal walking, with expensive perfume and wiping them with her soft and shining hair. Not again do the two sisters appear together in the inspired history. Indeed, Martha now vanishes completely from the Gospel stage.

And does Mary?

The oddly named problem of the three Marys has vexed the Scripture scholars for many a long century without moving perceptibly closer to a hard and fast solution. St. Luke tells us how, at some unidentified time, a sinful woman anointed our Lord's feet in the house of a Pharisee. John reports a very similar anointing by Mary, the sister of Martha, in the house of Simon of Bethany on the eve of the first Palm Sunday. Matthew and Mark both relate the latter event without naming the woman involved. Finally, all four Evangelists speak of a Mary Magdalen. The question therefore arises: Are the unnamed sinful woman, Mary of Bethany and Mary Magdalen all one and the same person, or are they two people, or are they three? Perhaps the puzzle is insoluble. We only mean to observe here that if Mary Magdalen and Mary of Bethany are different women, then both Mary and Martha disappear simultaneously from the Gospel story. If Mary of Bethany is Mary Magdalen, where was Martha while her sister stood on Calvary and watched our Savior die?

Cheerfully we leave this secondary Gospel problem to tease new generations of hard-working scholars and we turn our attention to the most certain and most prosaic common fact about these two women who were so dear to the Heart of Christ. We know that Martha served our Savior's dinner and that Mary anointed our Savior's feet. About Mary and Martha together we know just this: they were somebody's sisters.

We would very much like to talk about sisters. Not about nuns, who are the prized Sisters of all of us, but about natural sisters, to whom, naturally, no one ever pays any attention.

Think, for a moment, of the various roles played by women on the great stage of this world. Women are fair maidens, daughters, sweethearts, wives, mothers and grandmothers. Women are nurses and social workers and teachers and stenographers and tennis champions and actresses and, latterly, doctors and lawyers and diplomats and business executives, to say nothing of being natty Wacs and Waves and Spars. If the patient reader will pause to glance again through that catalogue, he will perceive at once that in every capacity named and in many another, women have attracted admiring attention. There is a useful modern noun which has been made to yield a much used modern verb, and both may serve us well in the present connection. In almost every part women play in human existence there is a pronounced element of glamor, and so modern woman has been industriously and successfully glamorized in practically every garb she wears, and under nearly every title she enjoys. The one woman who never rates a second glance is the girl whose only claim to notice is that she is somebody's sister. If, of course, she happens to be a strikingly attractive girl, if she is what is now elegantly termed a slick chick, she will unquestionably receive a second glance and more. But notice: at that second glance she passes magically, in the glancing eye, from the category of being someone's sister, and pops into one of the classifications enumerated above.

Does anybody remember reading a novel or seeing a play or sitting through a movie in which the heroine was the heroine on the strength of being a devoted sister? Has the film been produced in which the wild young wastrel returns, in a last touching scene, to throw himself in sorrowful gratitude at the feet of the sister who alone continued to believe in him when all others had given him up, and who devoted her life to his reclamation and rehabilitation? No, that film has not been made, nor will it be made. No one wants to sit and watch in a movie what he can see almost any time by just looking about the neighborhood in which he lives.

In a way, it is odd that the sisters of this world hold so little appeal for the poets and the story-tellers and the musicians of this world. For the average sister is brimful of the very commodity which is supposed to spark and inspire the artist. Sisters are generally people full of love. The difficulty, of course, is a most familiar one. Love is a terribly misunderstood phenomenon.

It would be interesting to choose, haphazard, a hundred men and women of different ages and conditions and with them conduct the familiar psychological experiment of instantaneous association. Mention to each of the hundred the single word *love* and see what word he (she) would immediately respond with. Most people would

probably answer with *sex* or *sweetheart* or *mother*. Some
might say *baby*, in one sense or another. A few might
think of *God* or *country*. Five will get you fifty, as the
racing fraternity puts it, that no one of the hundred subjects will reply with *sister*.

The fact is that in the much-abused contemporary mind
glamor is connected somehow with love as it is popularly
understood, and popular love is invariably connected
with sex or, at best, with strong feeling. Since no normal
man thinks of his sister in terms of sex, and since the
average man commonly regards his sister with no particular feeling at all, the male of the species does not
ordinarily associate the notion *love* with the notion *sister*.
It is all very understandable. It is all also quite spectac-
ularly wrong.

No one on the face of the earth loves more truly than
a sister, because no one loves so unselfishly. The expectant
mother fiercely loves the infant in her womb, and the
engaged fellow loves the girl of his choice, but nothing
could be more obvious than the fact that both stand to
get something for their love. A sister loves her brother—
or her sister—and stands to gain nothing. She just loves.
She simply gives; she rarely gets.

That is to say, a sister rarely receives anything either
very tangible or even intangible in return for her devotion.
It is perfectly true, of course, that sisters, like any other
relatives, or, for that matter, like anybody else, can become a nuisance with their attentive and too energetic
affection. It is likewise true that sisters, like all women,
will run any man insofar as he allows himself to be run.
But the explanation of both these difficulties is the same,

and it is itself a tribute to sisters. The love of sisters is love par excellence not only because it is utterly unselfish but because it is quite appallingly practical. Sisters do not romance, they simply and clearly love. Love of this sort is really terribly literal, terribly uncompromising, terribly free from deception, falsehood, hypocrisy and nonsense. Sisters love in the shockingly primary sense of desiring only and wholeheartedly what is truly good for the person loved. They can be wrong in their judgment as to what represents the true good of the brother or sister. Usually they are right.

Precisely because their love is so pure, sisters shoulder —and, as usual, nobody notices—a generous portion of the world's suffering. It is easy to think at once of three ways in which sisters in a family suffer far more than their brothers.

First, sisters agonize to a surprising degree over a moral defection in the family. We all know how heartbreaking for parents is the scandalous behavior of their sons and daughters. Our hearts go out in pity to the mother of the drunkard or the jailbird, to the father who must burn with shame at the mention or thought of his boy or girl. We Catholics are sadly familiar with the sorrow of the good parents whose son or daughter has married outside the Church. What we do not always notice is the degree in which such anguish is shared by the sisters in the family. Brothers will be shocked and angered and disgusted when brother or sister goes off the deep end, morally, and they will complain loudly and sincerely enough to all who will listen. Yet brothers are but men, and, man-like, they will shortly turn their attention to the endless urgency of earning a living, to the problems of their own families if they are married or to the fascination of their work if they are not. Man-like, they will soon forget. Sisters never forget a shame in the family. Sisters never give over waiting for the wilful wanderer to return. Sisters never fail to offer their own innocent reparation for the evil which they feel as theirs because it is the evil of their family.

In much the same way, death in the family, though it falls on brothers and sons like the heavy blow that it is, utterly crushes and desolates the sisters and daughters. It is wholly inadequate to explain away such an obvious fact by saying that women are more sentimental than men and that women's tears flow more freely. Whatever may be said about the tears, one wonders in his clearer and fairer moments whether women really are more sentimental than men. In any event, neither explanation touches the truth, for the truth is that women, and especially sisters, have a much more acute and sensitive and highly developed family-sense than even the best of men. When all is said and done, even a good man finds it difficult not to be finally selfish. Even a bad woman finds it difficult not to be finally unselfish. Almighty God's arrangements for life in this vale of tears are admirable even when they are not flattering. It is the task of men to pay for the fuel which keeps the *house* warm, but it is the noble work of women to supply the glowing heat, generated only in a human heart, which keeps the *home* warm. Mothers do this from the beginning. Sisters learn rapidly to do as much.

It is most strange, consequently, that the final frequent

sorrow of sisters in a family is the uniquely painful suffering of neglect. No one in the world is so easily overlooked
as a sister, and no neglect in the world is so completely
overlooked as this one. Because sisters love so purely and
because they commonly understand their brothers and
sisters pretty well, they are pained but not surprised by
neglect. They offer no protest, they raise no outcry. Since
brothers, at least, are apt not to observe an atmospheric
or psychological fact unless it sounds like thunder or looks
like lightning, the successive incidents or forgettings pass
without comment. So the familiar pattern gradually takes
form. The sisters in the family remember all the birth-
days, wrap all the packages, spend an annual fortune on
brothers, married sisters, nieces and nephews, clean the
house, cook the food, check the menu for the favorite and
expected dishes, make the last-minute, almost forgotten
phone calls, buy the theater tickets, consult the time-
tables, substitute instantly for anyone who is suddenly
prevented from doing anything, and do all this with effi-
ciency and dispatch, with smiling and unfailing cheerfulness. And which of us ever particularly pauses to say
Thank you, you've been swell, or to send a flower which
they can put on the table?

We brothers have three sisters as we make our laborious way through this world, and they all serve us most
nobly. There is the sister who is married, and whose home
is our home. There is the sister who is now everybody's
sister, because her name in religion is Sister Mary of
Something Lovely. There is the sister who, as we say
easily, is still at home. They all have this in common: they
are terribly devoted girls, and if their great love wins

little return, we can always console ourselves by recalling cheerfully that they never expected any return, anyway. Still—it might be nice to give them a thought now and again. They'll be surprised, but they will be mightily pleased.

Christ Jesus, born of a Virgin Mother, had no sisters, so He seems to have adopted at least two. Some of us are richer, in more ways than one, than the blessed Son of God was in His little day among us.

"Thereupon the mother of the sons of Zebedee . . . said to Him, Here are my two sons; grant that in thy kingdom one may take his place on thy right and the other on thy left."

MATTHEW 20:20-21

XV

MRS. ZEBEDEE

Whatever else the house of Zebedee may have been, it certainly couldn't have been dull. And you find yourself wondering who the head of the house really was.

Sometimes, as you read and reread the New Testament, you begin to wonder whether a Christian strictly needs to read any other book for any purpose whatever. If a man is looking for inspirational reading, the whole of the New Testament is obviously his dish. If I hanker for biography, the four Gospels offer me not merely the story of *a* life, but the story of *the* Life. If my taste runs to exciting adventure, there is the Acts of the Apostles. If anyone would like to dip into moral philosophy or listen to a stirring speech, he has his choice of the supreme wisdom and subtle eloquence of Christ our Lord or the slam-bang imperatives and roaring oratory of St. Paul. If you crave short stories you can always read our Savior's parables or the exciting tale that takes up St. John's entire ninth chapter, and if it's mystery you wish, try the same author's Apocalypse. Even if a man be in a mood for comedy, the New Testament, if closely read, will not let him down. The dry and subtle humor of Christ our Lord glints here and there in the Gospels, notably in His dealings with the twelve Apostles, and surely anyone would laugh at the incident of Peter and a none-too-bright girl named Rhoda, as recorded in Acts 12:12 and following. And then there is the celebrated affair of Mrs. Salome Zebedee.

By the early days of March in the last year of our Savior's life, it must have been clear not only to the Apostolic College but to our Lord's whole entourage that some very grave event was growing imminent, that some break must soon occur in their general situation. The general situation at the time was anything but good. To begin with, up north in Galilee, where alone pro-Christ sentiment had ever really amounted to anything, the whole movement, which had reached a peak of wild excitement immediately after the first multiplication of loaves and fishes, had simply collapsed. The thing had not exploded; it had only died, as a modern poet would have said, not with a bang, but with a whimper. In influential Judea, the true center of Israel, where Christ never had been popular, powerful opposition had been growing more overt and more organized until the electric resurrection of Lazarus had brought about the quiet but deadly caucus mentioned in St. John's eleventh chapter. That meeting of Caiphas and his friends had secretly marked our Savior for death, and possibly also engineered some official excommunication of our Lord from the synagogue and from all normal Jewish life. At any rate, our Savior had again slipped out of Judea, recrossing the Jordan into that same Perea where He had already been living quietly—almost what we would call *hiding out*—for several months. With new concentration He intensified the training of the special Twelve, He multiplied instructions and parables as if He were working against time, and we may reasonably guess that He grew steadily more preoccupied and grave.

All of this came to an abrupt end in a manner marvelously described by St. Mark. Our Savior suddenly announced to His followers that they would go up to Jerusalem, and His followers very definitely hesitated about following Him on such a manifestly foolhardy expedition. They were first incredulous, then flatly reluctant: St. Mark shows us our Lord striding along the Jerusalem road alone and well ahead of all the rest; next come the troubled and bewildered Apostles; the rest of Christ's party, openly scared, bring up the rear. With what looks like a kind of terrible urgency our Lord finally drew aside the twelve Apostles and in the most undisguised, circumstantial, shocking terms, told them of the dreadful tragedy that lay ahead in Jerusalem. On most of the Twelve the effect of this appalling communication was only deeper mystification and dismay. On the Zebedee family, however, the effect was more positive. Rightly reading this frightening prophecy in the context of the whole ominous series of events extending over the past half-year, the wife of Zebedee and her two sons decided that there could be no more delay, that the time had come for a bold and daring stroke in the interests of the kingdom of God and the family of Zebedee, especially the family of Zebedee.

The move that followed must surely have been the fruit of long if not inspired planning. Salome and her two boys not only act in careful concert, but with elaborate and cautious ceremony. They must surely have talked over, perhaps repeatedly and at length, what they were after, and what they intended to do in order to get what they were after. The clear marks of preference and preferment extended by Christ to Simon Peter, particularly during the past year, since the momentous and celebrated promise of the primacy at Caesarea Philippi, had certainly not been lost on the Zebedee family. It stands to reason that mother and sons must often have talked, in the friendliest way, about the possibility and the means of torpedoing Simon Peter.

Now the interesting question, "Who was the prime mover in this whole business? Did the mother work on the sons, or did the sons make a tool of their mother?" seems pretty well answered by the whole tone and context of Matthew's eye-witness account. It is Salome who is said to approach our Lord; the boys simply come *with* her. It is Salome who alone is described as falling to her knees. It is Salome who does the talking, who voices the daring petition. Even the fact that our Savior addressed His reply entirely to the pair of Apostles would seem to indicate that our Lord clearly recognized the real protagonist in this comedy and was subtly rebuking the leading lady for her volunteer performance. We may reasonably suppose, therefore, that in the planning which preceded this delightful event the stalwart mother had played Lady Macbeth to the twin Macbeth of her sons. It might certainly be urged in defence of Salome that she was ambitious for her sons, whom she loved, rather than for herself. Lady Macbeth was likewise undoubtedly ambitious for her husband, whom she loved deeply, rather than for herself. We can only respond in a dispirited sort of way that the contention makes no difference, one way or another. If a woman is ambitious as Salome and Lady Macbeth were ambitious, it really doesn't matter *why* she is thus ambitious.

At any rate, the little comedy began with the ceremonial entrance of the lady protagonist and the chorus, the chorus being the two boys. And first, the lady did something which the Greek translation of Matthew describes in a striking word. The root meaning of the compound word means *to kiss*: not in the Occidental romantic sense, but in the Oriental sense of giving a sign or mark of extreme veneration mingled with profound affection or love; we think at once of the kiss of Judas in the sorry Garden. In the compound form which our text employs the verb describes in the first place the deferential gesture of kissing one's own hand and extending it in veneration to a superior person. The wider meaning of humbled veneration in any external manner would follow easily. Salome prostrated herself before our Savior, whose blessed face I would love to have seen at the moment (or at any other moment), she kissed the ground at His feet, perhaps she borrowed a leaf from a more famous woman's book and repeatedly kissed the feet of Christ. She murmured that she wanted something.

Our Savior's answer to this somewhat general petition was cautious and eminently sensible. He said, *What do you want?* I imagine that John and James held their breath—surely by this time they must have felt rather like fools!—and that their mother took a deep breath. Then the petition poured out: *Here are my two sons.* (Our Savior must have thought to Himself: *Yes, I know. I can see them, and I know who they are.*) *Grant that in Thy kingdom one may take his place on Thy right and the other on Thy left.*

So there it was. Our first thought is to wonder what Salome would have proposed if she had had three sons; but we must sternly drag our frivolous mind back to serious business. Everyone who had ever listened at all to Christ our Lord was familiar with His plan and intention to found a kingdom, and everyone knew that this young Rabbi from Nazareth in Galilee was in fact claiming to establish that Messianic kingdom which was so familiar to Jewish thought. The Jews may have been and in truth were handsomely confused on the precise nature of this kingdom, but about the fact of such a kingdom there was no doubt whatever.

Now a kingdom meant a king, and a king in solemn state sits on a throne. Obviously, the choice, most important and most influential positions in the kingdom of Christ were the two subsidiary thrones located immediately to the right and to the left of the king. It must urgently be recalled that only a very short time before this present incident, in answer to a blunt, honest question from Simon Peter, our Savior had promised precisely this, that when He would sit on the throne of His glory, the twelve Apostles would sit on attendant thrones as judges over the twelve tribes of Israel. Salome was clearly moving in betimes on a very good thing. If there were to be twelve thrones around the main throne, two of those thrones were clearly the only two actually on the fifty-yard line, and it was up to her to see that those seats were reserved, not for that loud Simon Peter who was probably being pushed by that mother-in-law of his, but for her Jimmy and her Johnny. Dear Salome! I wonder what kind of life old Zebedee had. . . .

Our dear Lord's answer was, as always, perfect. He turned at once to the two boys, who, far more than their mother, represented His real interest and concern, and immediately began to talk again about His bitter future and their ability to share it with Him. Then He added, almost as an afterthought and surely for Salome's benefit, the ideal answer to her plea. He said equivalently, "About the seats, you'll have to see my Father." Having thus neatly disposed of the question, our loving and most lovable Lord presumably went on about His blessed business. Presumably, also, Salome got up off the ground and went on about hers. She was a good woman, and afterward would stand bravely at the foot of the cross, herself drinking deep of the bitter cup which Jesus had mentioned; but what would you give to have heard her that day as she stalked off with her Jimmy, her pride, and her Johnny, her joy? Or was she only thinking already, in her practical way, of how you go about getting an interview with our Lord's heavenly Father?

Such is the story of the little enterprise of doughty Mrs. Zebedee. Clearly, Mrs. Zebedee and her enterprise raise the whole painful question of the position of woman in the contemporary world and of the hotly debated attitude of the Catholic Church on that position.

Confronted by the whole fretful question of modern woman, that is, by the agitation (in both senses) of women themselves, by the ominous and very noisy feminist movement, by the spasmodic and even spastic literature on this subject, the average contemporary male can only exclaim, with a kind of exasperated bewilderment, *What do women want, anyhow?* A mere man's exasperation and bewilderment is endlessly compounded by a contention which appears in the very latest feminist book, a contention which effectively paralyzes the whole argument and which, therefore, some woman was bound, sooner or later, to make. It seems that there are men—described by one very peculiar book reviewer as "self-appointed specialists on women"—who actually do not qualify to take part in the debate at all: "legislators, priests, philosophers, writers, and scientists [who] have striven to show that the subordinate position of woman is willed in heaven and advantageous on earth." Besides, men had better beware of mixing in this argument: "No one is more arrogant toward women, more aggressive or scornful, than the man who is anxious about his virility." Now if, among men, legislators, priests, philosophers, writers and scientists are excluded from the feminist argument, and if any vigorous questioning of the feminist position can only mean that the questioner is nervous about his physical manhood, it can only follow that the feminist debate is now over, not because the women have won the row, but because the men have been disqualified from participation in it. If it be asked who disqualified the men, the answer is easy: the women.

This, dear and gentle and long-suffering reader, is the astounding argument of a feminist writer who, in the opinion and exalted language of an ecstatic reviewer, himself certainly not a bit anxious about *his* virility, thoroughly administered *his lumps* to such a tenth-rate thinker and bumbling logician as St. Thomas Aquinas.

Debarred as I am by my priesthood from the whole feminist controversy, I would yet beg leave of someone to admit that I am indeed anxious or nervous about this matter, though not, I urge with some embarrassment, in the precise way that the lady writer suggests. This harried writer really earnestly protests that he and many more like him are not worried at all about the virility of contemporary man. We are deeply concerned over the femininity of contemporary woman. And we do not quite see that we are being unfair or prejudiced or disrespectful when we ask once more, *What do women want, anyhow?*

If it be equality of human dignity that modern women want, they may rest content, because they have it. Especially do they have it in the authentic Catholic philosophy of life. From Leo XIII to Pius XII, that is, from the inception of the feminist movement until the present day, five modern Popes have repeated with unvarying insistence the Catholic doctrine of the equal human dignity of the sexes. Said Leo XIII: "The woman, because she is flesh of his [her husband's] flesh and bone of his bone, must be subject to her husband and obey him; not indeed as a servant, but as a companion, so that her obedience shall be wanting neither in honor nor in dignity." Said Pius XII: "In their personal dignity as children of God a man and a woman are absolutely equal." And again: "Man and woman are, in that which regards personality, of equal dignity and honor, respect and esteem." However, as everyone realizes, the feminist quarrel does not rage over some theoretical equality in fundamental human dignity, but about the practical application or implementation of that pleasing theory. Precisely here lies the root of the controversy. What is it that modern woman craves and claims as the concrete expression or proof of her theoretical equality with man? In other words, have modern women really thought the thing out, and are they sure of what it is they really do want in the name of equality? As a personal answer, this writer can only appropriate the saying of a justly cele-brated poet:

> *"I doubt it," said the Carpenter,*
> *And shed a bitter tear.*

Beyond any possibility of controversy, equality of the sexes for countless and (thoughtless) contemporary women means simply and purely the right to do whatever men do. Men smoke and therefore women must smoke. Men drink and therefore women must be allowed to drink. Men haunt taverns and therefore women may frequent cocktail lounges. Men sit at bars and therefore women will sit at bars. Men work in shipyards and factories, and therefore women claim the privilege—God help us!—of working in shipyards and factories. Men wrestle one another for money and television, and therefore women must wrestle one another for money and television. Men wear pants, so women have begun to wear pants. Now if this be equality, those women who want it are welcome to it. If it were not for the utter brainlessness of the whole ridiculous opera-tion, we men might be flattered as we never have been in all history. Everything we do, it appears, is simply ducky, and our opposite numbers can dream of no higher ecstasy than doing exactly as we do. That's high praise, lady; and if there were the slightest chance that you had any notion of just what on earth you are doing, we men might become even more hopelessly conceited than we are.

Of course, it will be urged that this is not a fair presen-tation of the case. The intelligent modern woman is not apt to hanker for the privilege of appearing in televised ice hockey because men take part in televised ice hockey. What the true contemporary woman asks is equality of opportunity where opportunity is really significant and rewarding: as in the world of business or of the professions. Why may not a woman today embark on any worthy career equally with any man?

There are really two answers to be made to this question. First, from every point of view, a woman may undertake a professional or business career; there is no prohibitive external obstacle. With the full approval of Church, State and society, and with, if I mistake not, the applause and admiration of all but the most misogynistic men, a young girl may nowadays set herself to become a doctor or a congresswoman or a business executive. If it be objected that in all such desirable fields of endeavor a girl is not really and completely on an equal footing with men, we can only beg women to be reasonably patient with the world in which they live, as they are so reasonably patient about so many things. It takes time for human beings to adjust to broad social changes, and the gradual storming of what had been the sacred world of men by the newly recruited and now fully armed Women's Auxiliary and Marching Club will need time for its general acceptance, especially for its general acceptance by women.

Certainly, as far as the Catholic Church is concerned, any modern woman who feels so inclined may embark on any career that is honorable and moral for a man, and God be with her. It is one of the oddities of this odd world that people take it for granted that the Catholic Church is opposed to careers for women, when the Catholic Church was offering striking careers to women in such fields as teaching, nursing, administration (St. Teresa of Avila), law (a beautiful Canon Law professor at the medieval University of Bologna had to wear a veil so as not to distract students during her lectures), government (St. Margaret of Scotland) and even diplomacy (St. Catherine of Siena), centuries before anyone else was allowing women to do anything but give pleasure to men and bear children. Exactly as great Chesterton noted long ago, those who hate the Ancient Mother invariably attack her with the wildest bitterness either for what everyone except herself has been doing for hundreds of years, or for what everyone else has been doing far less humanely than she. The older a true Catholic grows, the more clearly and serenely he realizes that his Holy Mother Church is never stronger, saner or more right than on the very matters wherein she is most savagely attacked. It is the old story: the Church provokes a certain class of people whenever she is wrong, but she goads them to foaming fury whenever, as not infrequently happens, she is right.

The other answer to the supposed special difficulties of women in the matter of careers is more subtle and therefore more difficult to express, at least in a way that will not seem prejudicial. A woman certainly *may* go in for a career; but *should* very many women do so? The point that must be appreciated about the present argument is that the argument applies to women generally without necessarily holding at all for any individual woman.

In the first place, unless this present writer is very much deceived, the majority of women still do not desire a career and never will. Next, it is as plain as a pikestaff—and someday when I have time I intend to find out what a pikestaff is—that the majority of women are not equipped for a career, and we beg leave to bypass the further questions of *why* more women are not fit for a career and what ought or ought not be done about it; let us confine ourselves to a simple *de facto* declaration of what seems so clear and certain. Above all—and here is the slight subtlety—human nature itself, and not any imperative of Church or State or anything else, indicates a marvelous natural division of the necessary chores and tasks and labors of this world by the different natural capabilities, aptitudes and inclinations of the sexes.

In all human history men have invariably fought the wars and women have invariably nursed the sick, not, as the furious feminists seem to think, because an early pope issued a Bull to this effect, but because nature herself makes some suggestion along these lines. Jesuits conduct colleges but do not ordinarily teach in grade school, not, as is universally believed, because they are so snooty, but because, being men, they are so inept for a job which the Sisters discharge beautifully, if not easily. It is one of the most rabid and yet reasonable convictions of many honest and fair-minded men today that if the true and essential tasks of women in our world are being neglected—and such an appalling social scandal as juvenile delinquency would suggest so—the basic reason is that nature's own wise plan for our race has been vitiated and upset simply because so many women are neglecting women's work in order to do the less important work of men. Someone sometime will have to lead me gently aside and slowly and patiently explain to me the ultimate mystery in this whole mysterious business: why women suffer so horribly from the most incredible and infernal of all human itches, the itch to stop being women and start being men. It is as if the rose were to try to become a cabbage, or as if fair Juliet were to long to grow a beard. Future historians may say that the men of our time were not really good. They almost certainly will say that the women were not quite sane.

The first time we meet Mrs. Zebedee in the Gospel story she is acting like Lady Macbeth. The last time we meet her she is acting like our Lady of Sorrows, for she is standing with the Mother of Christ at the foot of the cross. On the first occasion Salome behaves exactly like a feminist. On the last she is every inch a woman. So we will leave her, standing on Calvary where the faithful women bravely gathered and where the men were not. We are not laughing at her any more. She got over her itch for a throne, and settled for a cross. She proved to be a real woman and a real lady and a real saint, after all.

Epilogue

MOST BLESSED OF ALL

Of the scores of human beings whose common blessing consisted in this, that their mortal lives touched for a minute or more upon the mortal life of the Word Incarnate, we have called up in these pages a mere handful for our meditation and—fine old word—for our edification. The observant reader will have noted that almost all the people who have come in for discussion figured either in our Savior's childhood or in the early half of His public life. The fact is not accidental. As many such minor characters could be chosen, for similar reflection, from the last eighteen months of Christ's brief span of years.

Now, as the laboring scribbler comes gratefully into the twilight of the task he has set himself, he suddenly experiences a double twinge of regret. The writer finds himself unexpectedly in the position of a genuine novelist who for long has lived most of his working hours in the company of the characters he has created, and who knows, even as with untold relief he spells out the last pages of his story, that he will miss the people of his little world. For a long time now I have been living with these relatively unimportant men and women and children who dash in and out of the Gospel pages. They will forgive me if I say that I am glad to see the end of them, especially since they know perfectly well that I am going to miss them.

The other regret which this person feels is much more easily mended, and mended it shall be. These pages have necessarily neglected the Mother of God. Such unforgivable neglect may have been dictated by the nature of the work itself. However, let us take no more dictation of this sort.

Now once more, in the somewhat tense religious world of 1954, we hear raised against a most dear love the old evil cry of Mariolatry. There can be no question that one of the earliest and tenderest devotions of both the western and eastern Christian Church was devotion to Mary, the Mother of Christ. Nowhere and at no time was it even remotely suggested that the Christian God was not One in Three, but One in Four, the fourth person of the divine quaternity being not a god at all, but a goddess whose name was Mary. Every true Christian from the beginning worshipped and adored the omnipotent and triune God, Father, Son and Holy Spirit, but no true Christian in his right mind ever worshipped and adored the girl who became the Mother of the Founder of Christianity. There was always the feeling that the *Deipara* was the first and best and holiest and highest of all the saints, there was even a growing suspicion that the honor and reverence paid to her was somehow a little different from that given to the other saints not only in degree, but in kind. Nevertheless, no early Christian preacher or poet was ever heard to exclaim,

We adore thee, O Mary, and we bless thee, because by thy holiness thou hast redeemed the world, despite the fact that a sizable mass of reverent tradition early clustered around the Mother of the Savior.

On this body of venerable and persistent and invariably coherent truths the theologians of the Christian Church set to work, as they set to work on the entire unwritten revelation that goes by the name of tradition. By the Middle Ages the main outlines of an authentic Mariology were clearly blocked out. Then, awakened by the hoarse shouting of a frantic and frustrated German monk, the Reformation leaped snarling and clawing upon a somnolent Christian world. The new thing, which quickly slipped the control even of those who loosed it, snapped and tore at the Mass, at the Eucharist, at the Sacraments, at purgatory, at sacramentals, at celibacy, at the Papacy, at the veneration of saints, at so many gentle and holy realities. Then the reforming, bloodshot eye fell upon the cool, lovely figure of the Saint among saints. The beast went berserk.

The Protestant Reformation, which, with the passage of years, has softened its outcry to such a degree that prayers for the dead are now a commonplace of non-Catholic worship, has never relented with regard to our Lord's Mother. The most repugnant protest of Protestantism is as fierce and strident today as ever it was. One hundred years ago, when the Roman Catholic Church solemnly defined the dogma of the Immaculate Conception, Protestantism protested bitterly. Now the Roman Catholic Church, sure and serene as she always has been and always will be about her treasure of belief in Mary, has solemnly defined the dogma of our Lady's Assumption. Protestantism protests more bitterly than before: Mariology is nothing but Mariolatry in thin disguise. Now, however, aided by the unsuspecting and illuminating work of Sigmund Freud, Protestantism is in a position to explain *why* the Catholic Church is so hopelessly sunk in the swamp of Mariolatry. A celibate clergy simply must have some woman to love.

The present writer must freely admit that the first and most instinctive reaction of at least one Catholic priest to this explanation of devotion to Mary is indeed one of acute embarrassment. I am not embarrassed at having been found out. I am embarrassed as I am embarrassed at all the pseudo-Freudian talk of my sexual attachment to my natural mother; only much more so. I am also embarrassed that serious and decent and supposedly intelligent men of any religious stripe would think and talk in such terms as these.

The second reaction of the average Catholic priest to this malevolent charge is one of fast-growing suspicion. Such a small and tidy explanation of such a gigantic and complex fact as Catholic Marian devotion must strike any reasonable man as being altogether too pat. The whole position impresses as being, certainly, not too good to be true, but as being rather too simple and naive for unquestioned consumption. Is there nothing more to be said on a huge and ancient matter than this?

There is indeed something further to be said. One of the most aggravating characteristics of those who bait and hound Holy Mother Church is their unbelievably bland and impudent habit of proclaiming a conclusion about Catholic ways without the slightest regard for the actual facts involved. Has no one, for example, observed at all that nowhere has devotion to Mary been more emphatic and more tender than in the Eastern Catholic Church, whose clergy never was predominantly celibate and whose clergy is not necessarily celibate today? Has no one outside the Church no possible way of discovering or suspecting that the most enthusiastic devotion to our Lady burns not in antiseptic clerical hearts, but in the simple hearts of a non-celibate laity? In other words, on the sublime subject of the Mother of God do some Protestant apologists see with their eyes and think in their heads, or do they just foam at the mouth?

This much at least is certain: no amount of protest from anyone is going to discourage us Catholics, high and low, rich and poor, old and young, priests and people, in our fond and proud and joyous love of the peerless Mother of our Lord. Peculiarly constituted people may scream until the archaic welkin rings that we believe the most extraordinary things about lovely Mary, and we will answer happily that we only believe these amazing things because they are true. We believe that this priceless Maiden was conceived immaculate, that no least shadow or lightest breath of sin ever in any way clouded her spotless and radiant soul. We believe quite casually but with complete firmness that Mary remained truly a virgin while she became truly a mother. We believe that this wondrous Lady is quite literally and actually the Mother of God. We believe that the physical corruption which awaits every human body never in the least touched her unsullied body, but that our Lady, body and soul, sits as reigning and regal Queen amid the blinding splendors of heaven. We believe, as simply as any child reaching for its mother's hand, that the Mother of God is our Mother.

All this have truly Christian men believed and proclaimed from the beginning. All this will truly Christian men believe and proclaim as surely and as loudly and as lovingly in 2054 as in 1954. All this is the sheer joy, and by no manner of means the heavy burden, of Roman Catholic belief. We are not really angry at those who do not much care for our Mother and our Queen. We do feel very, very sorry for them.

This somewhat weary worker in words, as he turns away from the little people who have lived again in these pages, looks forward with eagerness to a future and everlasting meeting with many or all of whom he has written. He hopes to spend a portion of the long, bright day of eternity genially gossiping with old Zachary and Mrs. Zebedee and the forgetful disciples and the sisters of Lazarus and even (so kind and merciful is God) with Simon the Pharisee and the now sheepish men of Gerasa. But he will not see any of these, or know that they are about, until he has knelt in unutterable joy to kiss the gentle hand of Mary, the Mother of God.

Amen. So be it, *Deo juvante*.